The Language of Perversion and the Language of Love

THE LIBRARY OF CLINICAL PSYCHOANALYSIS

A Series of Books Edited By

Steven J. Ellman

Freud's Technique Papers: *A Contemporary Perspective*
Steven J. Ellman

In Search of the Real: *The Origins and Originality of D.W. Winnicott*
Dodi Goldman

In One's Bones: *The Clinical Genius of Winnicott*
Dodi Goldman, Editor

The Language of Perversion and the Language of Love
Sheldon Bach

Omnipotent Fantasies and the Vulnerable Self
Carolyn S. Ellman and Joseph Reppen, Editors

The Neurobiological and Developmental Basis for Psychotherapeutic Intervention
Michael Moskowitz, Catherine Monk, Carol Kaye, and Steven J. Ellman, Editors

Enactment: *Toward a New Approach to the Therapeutic Relationship*
Steven J. Ellman and Michael Moskowitz, Editors

The Modern Freudians:
Contemporary Psychoanalytic Technique
Carolyn S. Ellman, Stanley Grand, Mark Silvan, and Steven J. Ellman, Editors

The Language of Perversion and the Language of Love

Sheldon Bach, Ph.D.

JASON ARONSON INC.
Northvale, New Jersey
London

Chapter 1 was previously published in *Perversions and Near Perversions*, edited by G. L. Fogel and W. A. Myers. Copyright © 1991 by Yale University Press and reprinted by permission.

Chapter 2 was previously published in the April 1990 issue of *Psychiatric Times*, under the title "Narcissism's Expression May Be Mirroring or Identifying Transference." Copyright © 1990 by *Psychiatric Times* and reprinted by permission. It appears in this volume in expanded form.

Production Editor: Judith D. Cohen

This book was set in 12 pt. Garamond, and printed and bound by Book-mart Press of North Bergen, NJ.

Library of Congress Cataloging-in-Publication Data

Bach, Sheldon.
    The language of perversion and the language of love / Sheldon
Bach.
        p.   cm.
    Includes bibliographical references and index.
    ISBN 1-56821-262-3
    1. Object relations (Psychoanalysis)   2. Love.   3. Person schemas.
    I. Title.
    RC455.4.O23B33   1994
    616.89'17—dc20
                                                                    94-7906

        ISBN 0-7651-0230-4 (softcover)

Printed in the United States of America

For Phyllis, Rebecca, Brendan,
Matthew, Julia, and Sonja

CONTENTS

FOREWORD

THE LANGUAGE OF PERVERSION and the Language of Love by Sheldon Bach sets the standard for what we are trying to accomplish in the present series. While he is broadly a contemporary Freudian, Bach integrates and consolidates perspectives from a wide variety of theoretical orientations. He continues to expand and solidify the clinical discoveries that he first described in his previous volume *Narcissistic States and the Therapeutic Process.* In this book, Bach returns to the early roots of the Freudian literature; we are taken into a world that we had known about before, but now we are peering out from the inside. Bach is able to capture the world of fluctuating states, oscillating moods, and self values that ascend and descend, at times in chaotic fashion. We enter into an empathic bond with the book and with the patients who come alive for us in the course of the therapeutic interventions. What is remarkable is the author's ability to provide a theoretical structure that enables us both to better understand our patients and to place some of our own concepts on this scaffold. I invite you to partake in the illuminating and exciting event that is the reading of this manuscript.

—Steven J. Ellman, Ph.D.

ACKNOWLEDGMENTS

MY PRIMARY DEBT IS TO the patients and students who have taught me most of what is here, and especially to those who have graciously given permission to use material we have worked on together. I am also deeply indebted to my peer group, Drs. Norbert Freedman, Mark Grunes, Martin Nass, and Irving Steingart, who have been generous with both their time and ideas. We have been meeting now for more than thirty years in the closest I have come to a Platonic symposium, as we help each other digest the feast of experiences, both disturbing and exhilarating, that make up our psychoanalytic lives.

I am profoundly grateful to Drs. Steven Ellman and Lester Schwartz, who not only read the manuscript and encouraged me but freely offered me their scholarship, wisdom, and life support in ways beyond the call of friendship. I would also like to thank Dr. Michael Moskowitz, who so gracefully wore the double hats of colleague and editor. And, finally, I cannot adequately express my debt to my wife, Dr. Phyllis Beren, whose personal help and clinical good sense were indispensable and without whom, in fact, very little would have been possible.

INTRODUCTION

To define force—it is that x that turns anybody who is subjected to it into a *thing*. Exercised to the limit, it turns man into a thing in the most literal sense: it makes a corpse out of him. . . . Here we see force in its grossest and most summary form—the force that kills. How much more varied in its processes, how much more surprising in its effects is the other force, the force that does *not* kill, i.e., that does not kill just yet. . . . From its first property (the ability to turn a human being into a thing by the simple method of killing him) flows another, quite prodigious too in its own way, the ability to turn a human being into a thing while he is still alive. He is alive; he has a soul; and yet—he is a thing. An extraordinary entity this— a thing that has a soul. And as for the soul, what an extraordinary house it finds itself in. Who can say what it costs it, moment by moment, to accommodate itself to this residence, how much writhing and bending, folding and pleating are required of it?

Simone Weil, *The Iliad, or the Poem of Force*

From long before the Trojan War to the concentration camp universe of our own century, man has always possessed and often used his potential to treat another human being as a thing. It is this treatment of another person as a thing rather than a human being that I see as a perversion of object relationships and that forms the background of this book. Perversion in this sense is a lack of capacity for whole-object love, and while this often includes the sexual perversions, it also includes certain character perversions, character disorders, and psychotic conditions.) For as Freud noted:

> . . . it will be possible for the ego to avoid a rupture in any direction by deforming itself . . . and even perhaps by effecting a cleavage or division of itself. In this way the inconsistencies, eccentricities and follies of men would appear in a similar light to their sexual perversions, through the acceptance of which they spare themselves repressions.
>
> Freud, 1924, pp. 152–153

While Freud (1905) at first suggested that sexual perversions are the obverse of neurosis and may exist in people who are normal in other respects, I have found that sexual perversions are generally inconsistent with whole-object love or at least form a complemental series. Indeed, my therapeutic experience suggests that the developmental pathway to object love may be strewn with outgrown and discarded sexual perversions. But whether a sexual perversion *per se* exists or not, the question of how it happens that one person can degrade another to the status of a thing seems to me an issue of importance not only for the psychoanalysis of character but for our larger understanding of human nature as well.

In the first chapter, prepared for a conference on perversions, I consulted my clinical experience of patients with perversions to discover what they seemed to have in common(I found that though all of my patients had beating fantasies, what they also seemed to have were problems in separation and individuation, notably early problems in separation from the mother and subsequent problems of separation and boundaries in their later loves. I attempted to show the connection between the instinctual phase manifestations of the beating fantasy and the object relations implications of separation and to show why the beating fantasy, although anal in origin, often reflects earlier problems of the separation-individuation phase.

In the chapter on the language of perversion, I try to define more clearly the thought organization of people who consistently use others in this perverse way, that is, as part-objects. Interestingly, my material did not suggest that primal fantasies differ in normal and perverted object relations, but rather that normal thought organization deals with these fantasies through symbolic transformations in a psychic space that allows for paradox and ambiguity.

In one sense, perversions are attempts to simplistically resolve or defend against some of the central paradoxes of human existence. How is it possible for us to be born of someone's flesh yet be separate from her, or to live in one's experience yet observe oneself from outside? How are we able to deal with feelings of being both male and female, child and adult, or to negotiate between the worlds of internal and external stimulation?

I have tried in this book to show how some of the paradoxes of self/other, subjectivity/objectivity, male/female, and instinct/object are negotiated both in illness and health. People with perversions seem to have special difficulty in dealing symbolically with the ambiguity of human relationships. For various reasons they have not developed the psychic space that would allow them to contain paradox, making it problematic for them to recognize the reality and legitimacy of multiple points of view. Thus they tend to think in either/or dichotomies, to search for dominant/submissive relationships, and to perceive the world from uniquely subjective or objective perspectives.

The chapter on narcissism examines these qualities as they appear in the narcissistic character who presents with grandiosity and object denigration, and contrasts this with the complementary narcissistic character who presents with shame and object idealization, both components of the complete narcissistic syndrome. What these two types have in common are problems with evocative self and object constancy: the grandiose type inflating himself to compensate for his fear of the object's instability, and the idealizing type inflating his objects to compensate for his fear of his own instability. This typology is, of course, based on the presenting clinical picture, since the complementary side is always present, just as in sadomasochism, with which it is intimately connected.

In this and the chapter on altered states of consciousness I distinguish between subjective self-awareness (the immediate experience of self as a center of thought, feelings, and action) and objective self-awareness (the awareness of the self as an object among other objects, as a self among other selves.) While subjective self-awareness makes us feel alive and important, it deprives us of self-reflection and self-knowledge. And while objective self-awareness helps us to know our place in the world and to reflect upon it, it produces shame and guilt. This human dilemma, which begins to afflict us when we recognize our image in the mirror, is reflected in the story of Adam and Eve and their shameful acquisition of self-knowledge. It can be seen most acutely in the narcissistic disorders that are attempts to evade the paradox by living primarily in either subjective or objective self-awareness. Thus narcissistic pathology entails a disturbance in the dialectic between the varieties of awareness, such as in the grandiose narcissist whose extreme subjectivity and omnipotent self-inflation minimalizes his ability to self-reflect and to view himself objectively.⟩

This led me to consider the problem of omnipotence, which one finds as a major component of all the perversions and character disorders. I try to deal here not only with reactive omnipotence (grandiosity) as we see it clinically in the adult, but also with the infant's need for attunement and experiences of omnipotence as the foundation of basic trust, and with the human desire for transcendence, each related in its own way to man's awesome power and ultimate impotence. For death is the leveler that haunts the narcissist's grandiosity and it is often the denial of this ultimate, fatal humiliation that fuels his refusal to see himself more objectively as one person among others.

But over-objectification can also be a way of turning a person into a thing by viewing him as though he were a specimen under a microscope or a teeming drop of humanity seen from another planet. By distancing, one loses empathic connection with another being and is able to commit the grossest atrocities with little human feeling. As a character in Sade's *120 Days of Sodom* remarks:

> And what after all is murder: a small rearrangement of matter, some changes in its disposition, some molecules that are disassembled and plunged back into the cauldron of nature whence they emerge some time later assuming another form on earth; and where is the harm in all that?

If over-objectification can lead to the most terrible inhumanities, over-subjectification can lead to other kinds of part-object relationships. I deal with one variety of this in Chapter 4 the conscious or unconscious search for the lacking maternal functions or environmental mother (Winnicott 1965). Here the longed-for maternal functions make their appearance in the guise of idealized imagoes, making the Other far more important than the self. Although this may resemble object-love by comparison with the distanced objectifications noted above, it is still a functional use of a part-object, and subjects one to attacks of rage and emptiness when the idealizations inevitably fail)

Indeed, the rage at early environmental failure is one of many factors that animate the ghosts, monsters, and vampires with which Chapter 6 is concerned. For the no-man's-land or transitional area between ever-changing boundaries seems to be peopled by other-than-human creatures, and the less coherent the self-boundaries, the larger the unknown territory in which projective creatures, both good and evil, may spawn.

In Chapter 7, "Being Heard," I offer some vignettes from analytic work with a woman where self-coherence was a leading issue and the creation of meaningful psychic space a major task. This is not an extensive case report, and the material was selected primarily to illustrate some points about psychic space and the growth of symbolic transformations. I hope it also illuminates the evolution of self and object constancy as it was met in this particular clinical situation. But attunement, like interpretation, is only one of a multiplicity of interelated ways, some yet unexplored or perhaps unknown, by which psychoanalysis promotes the growth of psychic structure and develops the capacity for object love.

Sometimes, as we listen to case conferences and reports of no matter what theoretical persuasion, we may be struck by the repetitiveness of the constructs used to explain every aspect of the human condition. Theory is both necessary and constricting, whether it tends more to the objectifying or the subjectifying end of the spectrum, each of which, as we have seen, can have its pitfalls. At various times in our clinical work we may find ourselves lost in the subjectivity of empathy or the objectivity of theory, either of which used exclusively may be a perversion of our function. And although psychoanalysis embraces in principle the goal of understanding a person rather than using him, it too can easily enough be perverted, as can motherhood itself (Schreier 1992, Welldon 1988).

It appears that human beings can be turned into things in a remarkable variety of ways, sometimes even without their conscious awareness. In a world where so many forces conspire to urge the language of perversion, it remains a task for the psychoanalytic clinician to insist on the language of love.

CHAPTER 1

Sadomasochistic Object Relations

We need, in love, to practice only this:
letting each other go. For holding on
comes easily; we do not need to learn it . . .
Rilke: Requiem

IN ONE OF THE MORE philosophical passages of the
Marquis de Sade's *The 120 Days of Sodom,* the Duke
reflects with sadness and resignation that people are
generally so difficult to comprehend. "Yes," replies his
friend, "most people are indeed an enigma. And perhaps that is why it is *easier* every time to fuck a man
than to try to understand him."

This aphorism of the Divine Marquis seems especially
appropriate for a discussion of perversions, for it speaks
to the regressive nature of perversion and thus to the
sadomasochist in each of us. No doubt it is easier to
exploit a person than to relate to him, for relationships
require a dialogue, whereas usage can be simple and
unilateral, requiring only force, intimidation, or cun-
ning. In this sense psychoanalysis may be viewed as the
opposite of a perversion, because in principle it embraces the difficult task of understanding a person

rather than using him, although it, too, can easily enough become a perversion itself.

I would like to talk about one of the more ubiquitous perversions of everyday life in which the individual, rather than using a fetish or fantasy as a prosthesis to replace a missing part of his ego, uses instead a mode of relating that one of my patient's called a "technical" relationship, one that falls under the more general heading of narcissistic object relations.

Of course, sadomasochistic relations may or may not include actual perversions, but they always include sadomasochistic fantasies that may be conscious or deeply unconscious. They cover a continuum of nosologies from the neurotic through the psychotic, but I believe they are developmentally related to the sexual perversions because, like them, they arise as a defense against and an attempt to repair some traumatic loss that has not been adequately mourned. This loss usually occurs in childhood or adolescence and may take the form of loss of a parent, loss of the parent's love through neglect or abusive treatment that the child denies, or a feeling of loss of the self through childhood illness, traumatic disillusionment, or overwhelming castration anxiety. In this view, sadomasochistic relations may be seen as a kind of denied or pathological mourning, a repetitive attempt to disclaim the loss or to repair it in fantasy, but an attempt that does not lead to resolution because in some dissociated part of the psyche that loss remains disavowed.

The issue is complex because we are dealing with the interdependence of drive and object relations, for if, as Waelder (1930, pp. 72–73) notes, "the act of love . . . comes closest to being a complete and equable solution of the ego's contradictory tasks . . . " then the failure of that act of love, as in a perverse relation, may be understood as a failure of multiple tasks in many lines of development. Here, I can do no more than touch upon some of these lines, each of which must be given due weight to achieve both a theoretically plausible and clinically successful outcome.

From a certain perspective, one might say that a person has a perversion *instead* of having a relationship. To the extent that a relationship is pathologically defective and lacks the capacity for whole object love, we may say that a perversion or a character perversion exists. But just as perverse drive gratification may be a flight from intimate object relations, so perverse object relations may defend against anxieties about drives.

Regarding the severity of sadomasochistic pathology, a distinction might be made between those cases where the preoedipal and oedipal struggle with the parents has been over instinct prohibition and those cases where the struggle has been over recognition of the self. Cases where the parents condemn the behavior but recognize the child as a separate entity tend to fall into the range of neurotic perversions, and often enough the instinctual condemnation illuminates rather than eliminates the ego—"Your instincts are terrible but there *is* a you there." On the other hand, cases of parental nonrecognition, emotional absence, or a lack of mutual pleasure between parent and child force the child to flee to the sadomasochistic drives in an effort to deny the loss and to buttress a failing sense of self. Let me start with an example of this latter type:

A young man whose chief complaints have been chronic depersonalization and an unbroken series of sadomasochistic relationships with women reported with some astonishment that he was learning to cuddle and fondle his friend's children, something that he didn't know how to do before the analysis. He was astonished that they liked it so much and realized that he had never been cuddled himself and that his own parents were remote and distant. He remembered how afraid he was as a child to ask for anything and convinced that he must do everything for himself.

I noted that he still has ways of doing things for himself when he needs fondling, like masturbating or getting high on drugs.

He said he can't believe that anyone would want to love him, which is why in sex he ties women up and forces them to love him and makes them come even when they don't want to. . . .

There was a long silence, and then he observed in a tone of awe that a strange image had come into his mind of someone lying there screaming . . . being beaten up . . . a memory of crowds coming to watch someone broken on the wheel . . . someone being beaten to death with a stick . . .

I said that's just like cuddling and fondling, but with a minus sign in front of it.

He answered after a while that the most personal relationship he ever had was when his father came after him with a whip to beat him. "I really had his exclusive attention then, like I never did at any other time. . . . It's just like in my fantasies when I force women to have sex with me and to like it too. . . . I suppose you can get to like it if it's the only kind of fondling you've ever known."

In this way we arrived at the beating fantasy, the essential element of the masochistic perversion that Freud (1919) described seventy years ago. In that formulation, conflicts around oedipal wishes lead to an anal regression and the punishing and resexualized wish that we have seen: I want my father to beat me as a way of loving me. It is worth noting this patient's report that although his mother and father took good care of him, neither one seemed to derive any real *pleasure* from being with him, nor he from them.

A few months later this young man met someone on the street and became confused about whether it was me or someone who resembled me. He said that he could never recognize anybody, couldn't remember names and that he didn't understand what motivated people. He plaintively added: "I really don't know anything about people as human beings. . . . I just have a kind of technical relationship to them. . . . I don't know what you can do to help me . . . (?) Suppose I expressed sadness and you comforted me and I took that comfort . . . then how would I get up and leave? I can picture myself begging at the door—please can I stay—I can't go! At home there was nobody with the patience to listen. . . . Nobody sat with me as a kid. . . . And when I grew up in adolescence and someone listened to me sympathetically, I fell in love! . . . if somebody listened sympathetically, that's all it took. I tried to merge with them, to surrender all autonomy, and then it evolved into a contest—I'm controlling you, you're controlling me. . . . (How did that happen?) I would spend long nights with some girl and at some point it came to controlling them, tying them up . . . then I could play out the fantasy that she would always be where I wanted her to be and always accessible for what I wanted . . . and the less I knew about her the better, because if I knew who she really was it would make that fantasy impossible . . . if she lived in the real world she couldn't always be mine. . . . And that must be why I didn't recognize you on the street! . . . you're supposed to be here in your office waiting for me always and not running around West End Avenue. . . . ''

At this point we were able to do some work on how he ties me up in the transference by maintaining a "technical" rather than a personal relationship, keeping himself distant, tantalizing me with half-truths, forcing me to wait on his pleasure, and frustrating my therapeutic efforts. Over the next few years we saw this theme in its transformations as an expression of oedipal rivalry and aggression, as a defense against homosexual impulses and the wish to be beaten, as a defense against castration anxiety and a means of enhancing his potency, as a way of firming up ego boundaries and reviving a failing sense of self, and as a participation in the primal scene. No one of these perspectives or interpretations magically undid the problem, which was molded into his character and ego pathology, and I continually had to remind myself that in such cases we are attempting no less than to help someone separate, maintain object constancy, and achieve whole object love.

It is worth noting the vicissitudes of this patient's attempts to love. Starting from a situation in which he experiences both parents as unrelated and dead, through some combination of his projected rage and their own failure, he provokes his father into beating him not only as a defense against this rage and a punishment for oedipal wishes, but also to keep his father and himself *in love,* to revivify their relationship. In adolescence he falls in love with anyone who listens sympathetically, tries to surrender to them, and "and at some point it came to . . . tying them up. . . . Then I could play out the fantasy that she would always be where I wanted her to be and always accessible for what I wanted. . . . " The attempt to love has somehow miscarried and become instead an attempt to control, and although the patient is aware that this is only a fantasy, he prefers it to reality.

Because it may not be entirely clear how the attempt to love becomes transformed into a sadistic fantasy that glues both participants together, perhaps we can look at the beating fantasy from what appears to be the other side:

A young woman with a disturbed maternal relationship who had also been beaten by her father seemed to be forever in search of some kind of symbiotic experience. As we worked on this she explained:

"It's like when I ask to be blindfolded in sex and tied up . . . if I'm blindfolded I can imagine that he's tuned in right along with me whereas in reality you can see how he's *not* with you more than he's with you . . . the fantasy is, he will take care of you, will feed you, wash your hair, dress you, . . . you can just *be,* it's a fantasy of being perceived in one's essential being . . . the enigma and the indirectness leave room for the fantasy of being understood. . . . And the other thing about that fantasy is that it can never be satisfied . . . you have to keep it in that charged space between people that's never fulfilled . . . [How do you mean?] I don't feel perceived in the act of consummation the way I do beforehand . . . before *it's the apex of power,* it's all charged . . . they can consummate with any other woman . . . but not with me. . . . I retain my uniqueness because they're still interested, and there must be something special in me to keep them from going where they can be gratified. . . . "

With this patient the teasing and castrating behavior was designed to retain a sense of power that the consummation would destroy because it would demolish her body-phallus fantasy, make *her* feel castrated and empty and make her in reality dependent upon an imperfect object. More concretely, she was trying to recreate a situation in which all her father's attention was focused on her, but to prevent a consummation that would feel like the longed-for but humiliating lash of his whip. "If I'm blindfolded I can imagine that he's tuned in right along with me whereas in reality you can see how he's *not* with you more than he's with you. . . . "

It is certainly striking how both these patients *insist* on their desire not to learn anything real about their partners or the analyst because their fantasies of being "tuned in," or merged with an idealized other become endangered by rage and devaluation if that other person is realistically perceived. But one of them also complains of his *incapacity* to know anything about his partner or anyone else. My clinical impression is that this latter complaint is also to the point and that some of these people cover their deficit in understanding others with a variety of defenses, just as someone who cannot admit he is partially deaf may pretend to understand, may read lips, claim that nothing is worth hearing, or become hypervigilant and paranoid. Thus, their deficit in understanding others may be patched over by their "technical" mode of relating, in much the same way as the pervert uses his fetish to patch over a deficit in the body ego. This mode of relating is both an adaptive way to deal with their interpersonal deficit and a defense against the rage and devaluation that would destroy the object entirely.

We should note the instability of the narcissistic position, since at one moment the patient is sunk in masochistic surrender to the idealized lover whom she *knows* to be a figment of her imagination, whereas at the next moment she is sadistically manipulating the same lover, willingly exchanging the pleasures of sexual consummation for the pleasure of sexualized power. These oscillations between masochism and sadism and between passivity and activity are typical of such cases, and one may also find masochistic content being expressed within a sadistic structure or vice versa. But for the moment I want to emphasize the alternation between reality and its denial in fantasy.

For however we may choose to conceptualize this phenomenon in which both the reality and its disavowal remain in conscious awareness, it seems true that in his *experience,* the sadomasochist feels himself to be living in two worlds: the fantasy world where he plays the *game of the idealized omnipotent self and object,* and the real world, which seems too dangerous to exist in. In the fantasied world of the idealized merger, the laws of space, time, and logic, which promote differentiation, are suspended: separation, death, and mourning do not exist.

With my own series of cases, discussion of this "two world" phenomenon almost always seemed to elicit material about the parents and some strange aspects of *their* relationship to reality. Let me give an example:

> A man who was in a state of tormented jealousy and paranoia that he knew to be unjustified said: "I know in the real world that my girl friend has a right to do what she wants to do, but that doesn't matter . . . there's a different world in which I live, where my feelings really are, and in that world she has no rights. . . . " He then remembered a time at school when he was caught breaking the rules and his mother had said: "I'll go tell the teacher what a good boy you are and he'll let you off." He had screamed at her: "Mom, join the real world, they caught me and now I have to pay!" His mother had, in fact, never joined the real world, but he himself had become a voyager between the two worlds of reality and omnipotent fantasy in order to stay in touch with her.

In 1940 Freud had remarked with some wonder at the pervert's ability to both affirm and deny the existence of the maternal phallus and had conceptualized this behavior as reflecting a split in the ego. Traditionally, of course, the fetishistic perversion and even the character perversion has been explained as due to the traumatic sight of the maternal genitalia (Arlow 1971), but I do not believe it has been adequately explained why this sight may be traumatic for some and not for others. From my perspective, one may surmise that in some cases the *whole* mother and not only her genitals has been traumatic or, to put it more concretely, that some of those children who find the sight traumatic have discovered not only a fantasied gap in the genital area but also an actual gap in relatedness, and that the child's entire psyche has been mobilized to deny and to patch over this gap. In certain cases one can regard this fantasy of a frightening genital nothingness as the ultimate body metaphor for a series of developmental losses culminating in the fear that there is *no one there* to love or be loved by and no possibility of finding some libidinal connection behind the screen of technical relatedness. These parents are the sort of people about whom one might say: "There's no *there* there." Let me give some examples:

> A woman with sadomasochistic fantasies, commenting on her mother's presence said: "You speak to her on the telephone and she's not there . . . other people say uh-huh or mm . . . mmm . . . or you just know that they're there, but with her you wonder has she left the telephone. . . . Is she gone? Where has she gone?"
>
> This same question—where has she gone?—became the leitmotif that was repeatedly acted out in the treatment of a man who said about his mother—"She was always absent in my presence." He recounted how his mother had sent him to a doctor as a youngster because he slept too much, but he slept to avoid the emptiness and the pain of her absence . . . he remembers the doctor asking him questions, but it was a useless experience because it was his mother who should have awakened him by asking him what was the matter or talking to him or being alive or present in his presence. . . . When he was a kid he used to miss her and ask over and over again where she was . . . where has she gone? He would read *Playboy* magazine to stimulate himself and keep him awake. . . .
>
> He remembered that he sucked his thumb for a long time; the thumb provided a good feeling of connection that he didn't have with his mother—at least he knew where his thumb was! It was like an addiction, and he gave it up only when he turned to masturbation and that was like an addiction, and then he turned to women, and now with his

current woman he is in a state of constant jealousy and driven to ask her where she is going and what she is doing and interrogate her over every detail even though it hurts them both, and when he sees that she is as miserable as he is, then he can stop because it means that she loves him. . . .

We may note again how the attempt to love miscarries, is replaced by fetishistic substitutes, becomes embodied in a merger fantasy that is thwarted and finally turns to sadomasochism in a tormented attempt to discharge the rage and regain contact through the induction of a mutually addictive sexualized misery: "If I can make you feel as bad as I feel, then I know that you love me and we can retrieve our lost togetherness!" The utter loneliness, misery, and despair of the sadist reaches its apogee in the mad acts of the Marquis de Sade or King Frederick Wilhelm beating his subjects while shouting—"You must love me!"—but both sadist and masochist form a couple united in a common enterprise, each seeking in their own way to complete themselves through the realization of a perfect union.

In this case it seems clear that the sadism is in the service of recapturing the lost object, aggressively punishing it for straying, and maintaining a sexual excitement that will keep both self and object idealized, libidinized, and alive, so that his mother will never again be lost or dead to him and he will never again suffer excruciating pain. In playing this sadomasochistic game, however, he avoids mourning the loss of his mother or renouncing her, which would be necessary in order for the frozen developmental process to resume.

You may wonder why I say that the patient avoids mourning the loss of his mother when I reported that from an early age he was already bemoaning her absence and frantically seeking substitute satisfactions to help him feel alive. In part, of course, this is a retrospective account and he became increasingly aware of the significance of his mother's absence only as analysis progressed. More important, he had split off a part of his psyche so that he could remain close to his mother in her own omnipotent fantasy world, whereas another part of him was strongly connected to reality. Thus, like the pervert who behaves as if he both affirmed and denied the existence of the maternal phallus, he behaved as if he both affirmed and denied the existence of a loving and idealized mother, and so long as this dissociation persisted, his mourning could never be complete. Finally, the very defenses that enabled him to survive this cumulative trauma kept him fixated at an anal-sadistic-rapprochement level: he denied his loss by constantly seeking and finding substitute gratifications, he identified with the lost object and became a loser himself, and, most important, he renounced the oedipal struggle by partially identifying with his mother and taking the father for his love-object.

Thus his masochism kept him attached to the *idealized mother of pain,* the mother who was never really there and whose absence was so excruciating, but whom he reactively idealized and was omnipotently attached to in his masochistic fantasies. His sadism, on the other hand, was a denial of his need for her, a manic assertion that he could be omnipotently powerful by himself but that, in the end, was a primitive identification with the aggressive, omnipotent, and androgynous mother of pain.

Most of the time such children appear to be caught in a double bind, because although their sense of being effective is *discouraged* so that they feel no power and no way of having any real impact upon the parent, their sense of omnipotence and guilt is *encouraged* so that they feel responsible for the parent's failure, depression, and rage. One then witnesses a pathetic situation in which the child or adult, even while being physically or mentally abused, feels that he has brought the situation upon himself but is powerless to effect any change.

It is sometimes as early as infancy that the fateful choice to live in pain rather than to lose the object may already have begun, a choice that the sadomasochist repeats at each developmental stage. There may be a history of early maternal insensitivity or deprivation resulting in head banging, hair pulling, skin problems, or eating and sleeping disorders, which can be seen as precursors of masochistic adaptations to the unpleasurable maternal dyad (Novick and Novick 1987). In addition, the environment may have conspired with some object loss through the mother's depression, the loss of a caretaker, the birth of a sibling, or a childhood illness, all of which may intensify the sadomasochistic struggle. The conflict achieves heightened impetus in rapprochement, when the basic paradigm of clinging or going-in-search (Hermann 1976) and shadowing or darting-away (Mahler 1972) becomes embroiled in the sadomasochistic refusal to resolve the conflict of separation.

This failure to phase-adequately resolve separation has important consequences for subsequent difficulties in handling the heightened sexual fantasies and excitement of the oedipal period and problems around integrating a sexual identity. For sadomasochism in the service of repairing narcissistic vulnerability is also fueled by the impermissability of healthy sexual expression, as could be clearly seen in one of my male patients whose mother had wanted a little girl and had taught him that his phallus and his phallic strivings were unacceptable. He retained these strivings through a combination of drugs, masturbation, and perverse relationships, in which the perversions could be viewed as an idealized or denigrated prescription for what was necessary to complete his sexual identity and sense of self. It may be that one of the reasons we see fewer classical perversions these days is not only that social opportunities have expanded, but also that so many of these people now use drugs to help camouflage and patch over the defect in their ego functioning and reality sense.

This defect in reality sense or split in the ego, which is bridged by the fetish or ritual in the classical perversions, is bridged by the mode of relating in sadomasochistic relationships. And just as each fetish or perverse ritual must be unique for the bridge to hold or the patch to fit and function in the perverse act, so one finds a related intolerance for flexible behavior in sadomasochistic relationships. We may presume that this is a reflection of narcissistic intolerance for self–other differentiation as well as an anal omnipotence that declares: ''I want what I want when I want it!'' But the demand that everything feel just right is reparative as well, because in the childhood of these patients hardly anything felt right for them at all, that is, just as the patient was once a narcissistic extension of the parent, he now makes the partner or the analyst into a narcissistic extension of himself.

We may recall here Stoller's (1988) formulation that ''at the center of every erotic fantasy is a childhood trauma which is contained by the fantasy'' and that presumably guarantees its uniqueness. I believe this to be true also for sadomasochistic relations which are, after all, a way of loving, and that it is the combination of early separation problems with the unique traumata from specific developmental phases that characterizes these relationships. One might say that these patients have to some degree failed to adequately integrate the mother of nurturance and the mother of frustration, or the mother of pleasure and the mother of pain.

Ordinarily, if this integration has been achieved, then under the impetus of the incest taboo and castration threat the child goes in search of a replacement object to love. Going-in-search involves narcissistic affirmation in all phases, but also an acknowledgment of the reality of object failure and loss and the resulting anger that leads to a painful separation. This painful disengagement and symbolic internalization characterizes separation and differentiation, whether in rapprochement, in the oedipal phase, in adolescence, or in *mourning,* which is also a process in which the lost object is separated from by painful detachment and internalized.

It is precisely these painful detachments that the sadomasochist is unable to tolerate because his anger is experienced as an unbearably destructive separation from the object. Thus the masochist says: "Do anything you want to me but don't leave me," and the "anything you want" feels pleasurable because it means that his partner is still with him. The pain of suffering defends against the greater pain of loss.

The sadist turns this around and in a sort of temper tantrum plays at destroying the object in order to achieve pleasure, but it is only a false game because in the complicity of the perversions, the object is seldom destroyed or even harmed, while the pleasure of gratification through discharge only temporarily overcomes the pain of separation. Even in those rare instances where the object is destroyed, the identification with the lost object is often so extreme that suicidal thoughts and reunion-in-death fantasies predominate, as Schwartz and I have shown in our study of the

Marquis de Sade (Bach and Schwartz 1972). So if the masochist says: "Do anything you want to me but don't leave me," the sadist proclaims: "I can do anything I want to you and you'll still always be there!"

Thus the narcissistic sadist denies his object needs by overvaluing the importance of his drive discharge, whereas the narcissistic masochist denies his drive needs by overemphasizing the importance of his object attachments. Since the sadist and masochist are often the same person at different times or in different topographical states, sadomasochism may be viewed as a pathological oscillation between overvaluation of the drives and overvaluation of the object. In both masochism and sadism, however, holding on to the object typically wins out over letting go because at the stage of incomplete separation where the sadomasochist is fixated, letting go means losing not only the object but also losing a part of oneself.

It is in order to avoid this loss that the sadomasochist flees from the real world of dependency to the world of his fantasies where he can play the false game of the idealized self and object. I call it a false game because, as we have seen, it takes place in that split-off world of perversion that is acknowledged as both real and unreal at the same time (Freud 1940, Steingart 1983). But whereas the child's game is in the service of discriminating reality, uses the transitional object as a help in letting go and is on the developmental line toward independence and creativity, the sadomasochist's game is in the service of confounding reality, uses the fetish as a help in holding on, and is on the regressive line toward merger and stereotypy. The child's game involves *playing,* from which he may quickly make the transition to reality, but the pervert's game involves *play-acting,* never allowing the object to be real.

It is also a false game because it requires the suppression of real emotionality, especially anger, and the substitution instead of a "technical relationship," that is, a withdrawal of cathexes so that one is dealing with part-objects or self-objects in a world of one's own creation. In this world of dehumanized part-objects that is typified by pornographic literature, a regressive anal economy prevails: all objects are interchangeable and one can scarcely be distinguished from the other; the most horrifying sadistic and masochistic fantasies have no real consequence, and *nothing is ever permanently lost* (Bach and Schwartz 1972).

Unfortunately, in our real psychic economy, if nothing is ever permanently lost then nothing can ever be truly gained. For the price the sadomasochist pays by denying castration, loss, and death is to remain forever frozen into a lifeless stereotype that he is doomed to repeat. Where no loss, mourning, or renunciation is possible, then no progression is possible from one set of ambivalent life conflicts to another.

This fantasy of part-objects manipulated without loss unfolds in a world that the sadomasochist has split off or dissociated, in an altered state of consciousness characterized by extreme sexual excitement, sharply diminished reflective self-awareness, and a diminished sense that his acts are his own and under voluntary control. While in this altered state he feels as if hypnotized or in an *erotic haze,* and under its spell events take on a hyper-real and hallucinatory quality that make them seem larger and more compelling than reality itself. What I call the *erotic haze* serves to deny that reality is not in accord with fantasy, just as my patient had herself blindfolded in order not to notice that her lover was really *not* in tune with her. Variations on this denial range from closing one's eyes in sex or on the analytic couch to a characterological preference for the vague, the amorphous, and the ambiguous (Arlow 1971, Lewin 1948).

But in this state one also finds hyper-realistic imagery, images that in their hallucinatory clarity seem to deny that the object was lost and to proclaim instead: "No! It's not that she's gone! On the contrary, I see her more clearly and brilliantly than ever!" This is particularly striking in the works of Sade where the memory of his dead mother is transformed into that of a ravaged whoremonger whose image, in a moment of passion, becomes once again more glorious, bright, and beautiful than it was in life, a veritable resurrection of the dead imago. One recalls here the many visually concretized denials of loss in fantasy, from the luminescence of dead souls and the incandescence of the wake to the brightness of fetishistic perceptions and the screen memory (Greenacre 1968).

While the sense of voluntary action and reflective self-awareness *decreases* during the sadomasochistic act, the sense of aliveness *increases,* so that the patient feels he is being lived by his instincts or his id. The fascination of this regressive state is known to many, but it is especially attractive to people who feel chronically alienated, anxious, or depressed. In some cases this sadomasochistic sexualization defends against a profound libidinal deadness in the patient traceable to a defective libidinization in the early mother–child matrix. In other cases we can see how the idealization of the drives is used as a defense against the intimacy of object relations and the fear of loss, because to the

---

[1]See, for example, *Perfume* by Patrick Suskind and Chapters 4 and 8, this volume.

sadomasochist, the danger of losing his objects momentarily outweighs the fear of his drives.

Sooner or later, however, he begins to fear the loss of boundaries and becomes anxious and guilty about his omnipotent sexual and destructive fantasies. Many patients do not have the capacity to move easily from this fantasy world to the real world and to feel relaxed in both spaces: they cannot, as it were, get them together. It is important for the treatment to help such patients integrate these dissociated states of consciousness. But although it is essential that this split-off area be brought into the transference, analyzing it is no small task since it is precisely at this point of diminished reality testing and reflective self-awareness that the therapeutic alliance tends to break down.

In the area of the split these patients appear concrete, tend to view the world in stark either-or fluctuation, seem unable to comprehend ambivalence, and may have difficulty in appreciating that a single reality can be understood in different ways by different people. Since this appreciation of multiple perspectives is a basic prerequisite for transference interpretation, these patients have often been regarded as unanalyzable, oppositional or, in another sense, "perverse." The problems these patients have in differentiating and separating from their objects is reflected endopsychically in their inability to differentiate and separate from their own point of view or to take perspective on their own thought processes and thus to develop reflective self-awareness. In some ways it might not be misleading to compare sadomasochistic alternations and ambivalence to that of a person with pathological mourning, someone who frantically oscillates between believing that the love object is dead and believing that it is still alive, but who does so in such a way that true mourning never becomes possible. Thus, instead of mourning, we find a split in the ego, and instead of separation through painful detachment and symbolic internalizations, we find repeated attempts at reunion with the mother of pain through the false game of the idealized self and object.

For although, as Freud (1919) noted, sadomasochistic object relations are inextricably linked to beating fantasies, in many cases interpretation of the beating fantasies alone may not produce therapeutic success. In these cases there are difficulties on the way to whole object love, and I see the goal of analysis as *opening pathways to object love*. Let me try to sketch some implications for therapy that will be elaborated in later chapters.

Just as the child cannot usually develop object love without having experienced some kind of satisfying union with the mother, the narcissistic patient cannot develop object love without having experienced some deep trust in the analytic process as it is exemplified through the analyst (Ellman 1991). I am suggesting that, in addition to the beating fantasy, a more regressive fantasy of union with the omnipotent self and object must be analyzed and worked through before an enduring change can take place. The working through of this fantasy requires dealing with that split-off area of omnipotent objects that is defended by pseudo-emotionality and a frozen aggression that prevents separation and mourning from taking place. Once separation and mourning have been facilitated, the patient is enabled to again take up the developmental line of dependence–independence that had been blocked and replaced by sadomasochistic oscillations.

Another way of putting this is that these patients get better as they learn to be in a transference relationship that is not sadomasochistic? This is more complex than it may seem, however, because in the transference they do everything possible to subtly provoke either sadistic or masochistic reactions that are difficult for the analyst to discern, to understand, and to control. One sometimes sees in consultation cases where the sadomasochistic transference has been interpreted seemingly to no avail, or in which it has been jointly acted out in ongoing squabbles about who is going to control whom until both parties to the analysis have reached a state of mutual exasperation and exhaustion. Sometimes confrontive interpretations simply repeat the beating fantasy in another form, so that the patient is secretly gratified while being beaten with interpretations. This is but one situation in which the treatment itself can become a kind of perversion. To a certain extent, of course, incidents like this must be re-created before they can be understood, but the hope is that they will not be repeated indefinitely in the transference as they are in life.

In certain cases the analyst may not have fully appreciated that the patient's mental organization is in some respects still at a primitive level and that you cannot explicate the transference, which is a metaphor, to a patient whose mind cannot embrace the cognitive flexibility of metaphors. What this means in practice is that such a patient will confuse or confabulate what should be transferential and symbolic issues into *real* issues of love or death, and will struggle with you as if you were *in fact* trying to rape or kill him.

If certain of these patients are persistently confronted with the analyst's reality before a reliable autonomy has developed, then two perversions of treatment may ensue. In the first, the patient becomes acquiescent and agrees, but does not develop a genuine sense of self, and a prolonged pseudo-analysis results. In the second, the patient disagrees and eventually either leaves or conforms, but he becomes internally isolated, suspicious, and schizoid. He learns, in short, to keep his thoughts to himself and renews his conviction that there is no one in the world he can really trust and nothing to believe in.

Because the person with narcissistic pathology and sadomasochistic tendencies has never learned to trust his objects, he can never feel truly at home in the world. One of my patients constantly compared his life experience to that of a character in Hemingway who says: "When you're born they put you into the game and they tell you the rules and the first time they catch you off base they kill you." In the world of the sadomasochist there is no margin for error, no compassion, and no forgiveness. It is consequently very difficult to help these patients learn to love, to separate, and to mourn.

It seems that the sadomasochist interposes an impersonal or technical relationship between his desire and his object. This alienates him both from himself and from the object of his desire (Khan 1979) in the interest of denying his dependence upon objects that have failed him in the past. This denial takes the form of manic or grandiose assertions of exceptionality, perfection, and omnipotence, *the game of the idealized self and object,* which includes denial of separation and sexual identity, denial of loss and castration, and denial of helplessness and depression. The masochist's longed-for surrender to an idealized other, or the sadist's merger with his grandiose omnipotent self is the ultimate way of avoiding the ambivalence conflict between dependence and independence. One might say that in searching to avoid a real dependence upon an actual fallible object, the sadomasochist substitutes a fantasied dependence upon an idealized infallible object.

In this way, much like those political terrorists exiled from their homeland, the sadomasochist spends his days in fantasies of recapturing a lost Paradise that never in fact existed, while at the same time refusing to compromise by living in the real world that might actually be possible.

CHAPTER 2

Problems of Narcissistic Love

THERE WAS A TIME, just a few decades ago, when the leading expert on the treatment of narcissism kept a crown and scepter beneath his chair that he would present to his grandiose narcissistic patient at an appropriate moment. Most of us have abandoned this form of deliberate shock therapy because we have come to understand that the countertransference that produced it is in fact one of the most difficult aspects of the treatment and that, as Freud (1914) noted, our envy for the blissful libidinal position of narcissists, beautiful people, great cats, and children may account to some extent for our difficulty in empathizing with them.

This increasing understanding of narcissism has also widened our diagnostic net beyond the type of narcissist who presents with haughty grandiosity, a sense of entitlement, and shallow and devalued relationships, which I shall call the *overinflated* narcissistic type. Now we may also include in this category those patients who show the "other side of the coin" (Bach 1977, Broucek 1982, Gabbard 1989) and present with complementary feelings of inferiority and hypersensitivity, boredom and uncertainty, and chronic idealizations followed by disillusionments, which I shall call the *deflated* narcissistic type. One tends to think that the overinflated narcissistic type has too much pathological narcissism, whereas the deflated narcissistic type has too little healthy narcissism, but we shall later see that this formulation is somewhat oversimplified and that both types share a common defect of representational constancy.

Those overinflated patients who present with grandiosity and entitlement tend to form a mirroring transference (Kohut 1971), in which the patient insists that the therapist should *reflect* or mirror the patient's grandiose wishes; whereas those who present with depletion and inferiority tend to form an idealizing transference, in which the patient insists that the therapist should *embody* his grandiose wishes. While many narcissistic patients alternate between feelings of grandiosity and inferiority, the literature has tended to emphasize the grandiose or overinflated patient, sometimes reserving other diagnoses such as regressed oral hysteric, infantile personality, or masochistic character for the type who presents with depletion and inferiority. For a long time the treatment of the narcissistic disorders was embroiled in a lively debate between proponents of conflict and of deficit, but the passage of time suggests that framing the issues in these terms is not entirely clarifying, if only because it now seems apparent that developmental deficits lead to unresolvable conflicts and that unresolvable conflicts engender developmental failures (Auerbach 1993, Eagle 1984).

Although overinflated and deflated narcissists are ideal types reflecting only presenting aspects of the personality, I include both in the diagnosis of narcissism because I feel that the one is often simply the overt or the covert face of the other (Akhtar and Thomson 1982). Indeed, an important part of the therapeutic task consists in uncovering the sense of depletion and inferiority in the overinflated-type narcissist and in uncovering the grandiosity and entitlement in the deflated-type narcissist. I also include on this continuum certain patients with narcissistic character disorders who present with symptoms of perversion, addiction, eating disorders, or psychosomatic complaints, because I believe these are structurally related and therefore show a similar evolution in the transference and treatment. I might mention here my impression that these patients frequently show a history of unusual sensitivities as young children, so that they might require unusually nurturant or devoted parenting to successfully manage their unusual temperaments (Ellman 1992, Suomi 1991).

In all these conditions there appears to be a difficulty with evocative constancy, that is, a weakened capacity to evoke or hold on to the object representation when the object is absent, or to hold on to the self representation when the object is not there to sustain it. The overinflated narcissist is someone whose sense of his *objects* is fading and who compensates by overinflating himself and insisting he is so powerful that he doesn't need objects, whereas the deflated narcissist is someone whose sense of *himself* is fading and who compensates by overinflating an object and then clinging to this idealized figure for stability.

All these patients have related difficulties either with the immediate experience of themselves as the center of thought, feelings, and action (subjective awareness), or with the awareness of themselves as an object among other objects, a self among other selves (objective self-awareness). At first view, the overinflated narcissist has difficulty being aware of himself as an object in a world of other people, whereas the deflated narcissist has difficulty in the immediate experience of himself as a center of thought, feelings, and action. But both types have persistent difficulties moving back and forth between these two perspectives on the self and integrating them into their representational world (Bach 1980, 1985).

The normal or neurotic is able to experience both himself and his objects as cohesive and alive because in normal development the self and object representations grow and mature simultaneously, and self-love develops concurrently with object love. But in narcissistic development the overinflated narcissist can experience himself as cohesive and alive only at the expense of devitalizing his objects, whereas the deflated narcissist can keep his objects cohesive and alive only at the expense of devitalizing and fragmenting himself. Because self- and object constancy are the foundation of symbolism, these representational deficits have corresponding symbolic and cognitive deficits such as difficulties in dealing with multiple points of view, in tolerating ambiguity, and so forth. But before exploring how this develops, let me first situate this syndrome on the diagnostic continuum.

The narcissistic personality type can be distinguished from the borderline personality by his better functioning in the real world and by his more cohesive and integrated self- and object representations, leading to a greater degree of fused or modulated aggression. While in the borderline patient the aggression leaks out and can explode at any moment, in the narcissistic patient whose representational world and sense of self is more stable, the aggression is often linked to particular experiences of narcissistic injury and may yield to interpretation or repair of that injury.

The narcissistic personality disorder can be distinguished from neurotic disorders of the hysterical and obsessive kind by the development of a predominantly narcissistic transference, that is, a transference in which boundaries between self and object are permeable to a greater or lesser degree and can be seen to dissolve within the analytic transference situation, but rarely outside it. There are innumerable practical clues to this situation; for example, the narcissistic patient may often not bother to explain the context of what he is saying because he assumes you are either one with him or not worth informing at all, whereas the neurotic patient will generally tell you what you need to know in order to understand him. Thus the narcissistic patient may speak for days about someone before you discover whether this is a friend, a lover, or some former acquaintance; he may allude to people without actually naming them or allude to events without actually describing them so that after a while you begin to feel as if you too were living in a narcissistic haze and are somewhat disoriented as to time, place, and person. These are merely manifestations of the fact that the narcissistic patient's inner world is focused primarily upon himself or a self-object and that his whole-object relationships are weak and less differentiated.

I believe that many of the narcissistic disorders share a developmental origin in what I have called the anal/ depressive/ rapprochement/bisexual phase. This is the pregenital phase that includes Freud's anal stage, Klein's movement from paranoia to reparation and object-love,[1] Mahler's rapprochement sub-phase, and the bisexual flux characteristic of this period. This is the period when the toddler is first gaining objective self-

---

[1]I have, of course, advanced Klein's timetable while retaining her conceptualization, in the belief that this realignment is more in keeping with our current understanding of child development.

awareness, the ability to view himself from someone else's perspective, and when he is particularly vulnerable to experiences of humiliation and shame. Shame is the affect that regulates exhibitionism and self-esteem, and in helping to demarcate the boundaries of our difference and separation from others it becomes intimately linked with self and object representations. But even though the interactions at this time are particularly conducive to shame experiences and narcissistic pathology, subsequent developmental restructurings may alter or modify the outcome or may initiate pathology at a later time.

Frequently, however, one finds that events in this period have started a sequence of developmental failures, conflicts and regressions that give rise to the typical problems associated with the continuum of the narcissistic disorders. Some of these problems are:

A: *Disturbances of self-constancy and of self-regulation*

1. There is a subtle disturbance in the sense of bodily continuity so that the patient may experience his body as strange or different, shading into hypochondriacal preoccupations.

2. There is a subtle disturbance of the sense of mental and emotional continuity so that the patient may fear his thoughts and feelings as potentially unstable or subject to sudden and inexplicable shifts, that is, a mild person may momentarily experience himself as Frankenstein.

3. There is a disturbance of self-continuity across alternate states of consciousness, so that the patient's sense of himself may become fragile in states of fatigue, of high arousal, of intoxication, or in dream or dream-

like states. There are similar disturbances of the sense of self at moments of transition such as from waking to sleeping, on arriving or departing, traveling, moving, and so forth. All these disturbances of bodily and emotional continuity may be clinically hidden behind some simple statement such as "I don't feel like myself today." These transitional disturbances shade into:

B: *Disturbances of separateness*

These patients show anxiety at separation or an inability to separate or a difficulty in being alone, which in the deflated narcissistic type is often a symptom or presenting complaint and in the overinflated narcissistic type is generally handled by denial or counterphobic and manic mechanisms.

C: *Disturbances of object constancy and object relatedness*

One finds a certain interchangeability of objects, shallowness of object relations, or sadomasochistic object relations that tend to be manifestly sadistic in the overinflated type and manifestly masochistic in the deflated type, with the other side of the coin always present in the latent content.

D: *Disturbances of reality testing and of mourning*

The overinflated narcissistic type frequently displays a denial of his limitations, his finiteness, or his vulnerability; he has grandiose fantasies of brilliance, power, and entitlement, and he shows a persistent refusal to admit or to mourn the loss of his own omnipotence.

The deflated narcissistic type presents with the obverse feelings of inadequacy, extreme vulnerability, and depression and, while bemoaning the loss of his own omnipotence, he seems to be desperately seeking an omnipotent object to unite with, to idealize, and to appropriate its power.

E: *Disturbances of sexual identity*

Although sexual disturbances are most obvious in narcissistic patients with eating disorders or sexual perversions where they may be consciously acted out, at a less conscious level most narcissistic patients have a persistent desire to be or to become both sexes and they display sexual confusion and androgynous fantasies. This sexual confusion is related to disturbances of separateness and of self constancy, and to an omnipotent denial of limitations.

Diagnostically, one may divide the narcissistic continuum into higher and lower levels according to functioning, but this becomes confusing because of the often enormous discrepancies between the pathology of the inner life and the frequently excellent outward adaptation in this character type. If one were to make a division, I would prefer to make it in terms of those patients who are more or less able to accept symbolic rather than actual gratifications, a point of major importance as we turn to considerations of treatment, especially of the milder addictions and eating disorders.

Narcissistic personalities with addictions and eating disorders are the clearest examples of the disturbances of self-regulation enumerated earlier. The narcissistic addict, bulimic, or anorectic *is attempting by substance abuse to regulate his emotions in order to achieve a state of well being.* In successful psychoanalysis the patient becomes addicted to a human relationship instead of to a substance. This addictive relationship helps the patient manage his anxieties, depressions, and feelings of emptiness in a better way than with earlier objects and develops his ability to regulate himself and eventually to wean himself from the relationship. This therapeutic object relationship (Grunes 1984) offers the patient a chance to interact with a separate but constant object and to analyze his difficulties in handling both separateness and object constancy.

Although substance abusers and eating disorders offer the most dramatic examples, all the narcissistic disorders may be thought of as showing addictive tendencies. Thus the overinflated narcissist is addicted to a mirroring figure or "yes-man," while the deflated narcissist is addicted to an idealized other who infuses him with life, while both types show "withdrawal symptoms" when the self-object is removed. Such patients may become dependent upon or addicted to the treatment before they have developed real trust in the situation, putting them in conflict between their addictive needs and their potential vulnerability. The natural evolution of the therapy along standard analytic lines, by accepting the patient's projections and without any role playing by the therapist, results in the provision of precisely that sort of therapeutic object relationship that each particular patient needs. But analytic trust may have to be slowly established and then reestablished after each shift in the transference situation (Ellman 1992).

It is important to note that while the higher level narcissistic patient is able to use the therapeutic object relationship to help himself compensate for deficiencies of self- and object constancy and of self-regulation, patients at the lower level of the continuum may find it difficult to accept a relationship that provides only *symbolic* rather than actual gratifications. Because the development of evocative constancy underlies symbol formation (Auerbach 1993), such patients have not yet reached that stage where symbolic words replace enactments or acting out. An important treatment goal is to bring this about through a holding environment that provides a constant yet separate object, as well as through understanding, clarification, appropriate therapeutic responses, and, eventually, interpretation.

Although one may quite legitimately view the narcissistic disorders as deep characterological defenses against both libidinal and aggressive conflicts, I find that this conceptualization often leads to ignoring the basic disturbances of self- and object representations and evocative constancy and sometimes encourages premature attempts to break through the narcissistic defenses. Such premature confrontations often lead to narcissistic rage reactions in the overinflated patients and to a pseudo-acquiescence in the deflated patients, but not to structural growth. Effective interpretation of libidinal and aggressive conflicts becomes possible only as self and object representations become more differentiated, constant, and cohesive. This point is clinically marked when the patient begins to experience that *the same reality can be viewed in different ways by different people and that his point of view and the therapist's point of view can both have reality and legitimacy.* This is another way of talking about the attainment of mutual trust in the analytic situation (Ellman 1991), a trust that these patients lack and that must be affirmed and reaffirmed at different stages of the analysis. Before that time, interpretations of libidinal and aggressive conflict are often counterproductive and, indeed, may spring more from the therapist's countertransference than from the patient's needs.

Many clinicians agree that the countertransference is the major stumbling block in treating narcissistic patients, either because we cannot tolerate the consistent disregard shown for our human rights and our very existence by the overinflated, entitled narcissist, or because we cannot tolerate the idealizations projected onto us by the insecure and deflated narcissistic patient. It may help to remember that behind the former's entitlement lie profound feelings of inadequacy, and behind the latter's experienced inadequacy lie deeper feelings of grandiose entitlement. As the treatment progresses and the defenses are analyzed, these complementary sides should emerge, and ultimately the presenting distinctions between the two types should dissolve as a more complete human being emerges. Of course, no real-life analysis proceeds in so schematic a fashion since in analyzing the narcissistic structures and defenses we are simultaneously uncovering the libidinal and aggressive conflicts and dealing with them as we do in any ordinary analysis.

But as the dissociation decreases so that the patient feels *himself* to be more of a whole and trustworthy person, the patient also begins to experience the *therapist* as more of a whole and trustworthy object. Sometimes the therapist also begins to see the patient in a more complete way and, most interestingly, the therapist may feel that he himself has grown from the experience as his own countertransference splits have been dealt with and overcome.

One of the earliest signs of this growing trust may appear in the countertransference with the overinflated patient, when the therapist begins to feel that he is no longer walking on eggs, and that he can from time to time say exactly what he thinks without totally disrupting the treatment. Similarly, it is a sign of progress when the deflated patient can disagree and maintain his own position without fear, shame, or overcompensation. The emergence of a real dialogue between two separate people signals a new phase in the treatment, but this important goal may require considerable patience, understanding, and technical dexterity to achieve.

Trained as we all have been in a therapeutic model that assumes we are talking to another separate, distinct, and individuated person, it is often quite difficult to imagine the extent to which people suffering from narcissistic problems may live in a world of fusion, merger, and omnipotent fantasies. So it may come as an unwelcome surprise to both parties to abruptly discover that the person with whom we have been working for some time really does not share certain of our basic assumptions about how the world operates.

A few months ago I was consulted by a very competent therapist who had been treating a patient for more than two years with quite positive results. A problem arose when for the first time the therapist needed to change an appointment and offered the patient some alternate hours. Much to the therapist's surprise the patient, who was normally deflated and acquiescent, became outraged at the thought that the therapist could change hours whenever she wanted to, whereas the patient was obliged to conform to the therapist's availability when changing hours. The patient stated with absolute sincerity that she did not see how she could continue in treatment with someone who was so untrustworthy as to change an hour, although in fact the patient herself had frequently changed hours for business reasons, whereas the therapist had never done so before.

The therapist was stunned, as I have been in similar situations, at this unsuspected revelation of the extent of her patient's narcissistic vulnerability. No appeals to reason, no interpretations of the projection or of the transference, no parallels with any childhood feelings or previous situations were of any avail, and, with the treatment hanging in the balance, the therapist had come for consultation. With an increased understanding of what was at issue, she was fortunately able to turn the situation around, but we took the occasion to explore in just how many different areas the therapist's own assumptions about the world were not necessarily shared by the patient. We concluded that for a very long time she would have to make continual allowance for the fact that, in some way, she and her patient were living in different worlds (Bach 1985) that overlapped to only a limited degree. Each time that their worlds or perspectives clashed, analytic trust would be disrupted and would need to be slowly reestablished. This patient had felt throughout her life that if she made the slightest mistake her parents might discard her like a used Kleenex, and she was treating the therapist in much the same way. But it took a long time before this interpretation could be made.

The kind of incident I describe is, of course, commonplace to anyone who has worked with narcissistic patients, and one that frequently makes the therapist feel he must tread very gingerly. For no matter how many times we experience it, it is always a shock to our own narcissism to realize that another person who seems so like us on the outside may, on the inside, think or feel so differently from us.

It is at this point of the absolutely inevitable transference–countertransference crises that treatment techniques may differ. Instead of advising my supervisee to hand her patient a golden crown or to confront the irrationality of her behavior, I noted it was a positive step that this deflated and compliant patient's grandiosity had finally emerged, be it in ever so distorted a form, and I advocated treating her sense of betrayal by the therapist as a valuable and legitimate feeling.

I must emphasize that all attempts at analyzing the transference in a symbolic way had utterly failed and probably should not have been attempted, because the patient was clearly not yet able to understand that the same reality can be viewed in different ways by different people and that her point of view and the therapist's point of view might both be legitimate. I take it as an axiom that unless we first come to experience the patient's point of view as legitimate, not only as a transference reaction but also as an experiential reality for us, then the patient will hardly ever come to experience that our point of view can also be legitimate. We are looking, as it were, to enter the patient's world or psychic reality or to find the kernel of experiential truth in whatever his position may be.

If the patient is coerced, however subtle the method, into accepting our point of view without truly believing it, then his narcissism has not matured but has only been circumvented, and it is very likely to emerge again in distorted and unexpected ways. This situation is related to the unfortunate circumstance we used to encounter in training situations where candidates were assigned to an analyst, which sometimes led the candidate to conclude that his training analysis was "for the Institute" and that he would need a second analysis "for himself." I believe it of crucial importance for every person to have an analysis that belongs to himself and not to his analyst, no matter how noble and well-intentioned that analyst may be.

But I have mentioned elsewhere the dilemma involved in having to make this unfortunate choice. In principle the treatment should belong to both participants and be a mutually cooperative endeavor or, if not, that fact should be the subject of interpretation or of self-reflection on the part of the analyst. But for mutuality to exist we must have two participants who feel themselves to be autonomous people, capable of saying "yes" and "no" to each other while maintaining respect for each other's point of view. But it is precisely this capacity to form a mature object relationship, a working alliance, or a transference neurosis that is lacking in narcissistic patients to a greater or lesser degree, depending on the extent of disruption to their self-awareness and evocative constancy. A mature relationship and a true transference neurosis require both a self and other who are whole, vital, and unfragmented.

Clearly, the young woman who felt betrayed and ready to leave treatment because her therapist asked her to change an hour had not yet reached this stage of relatedness. And my point is that until she does, we are better advised to take our therapeutic stance within her world rather than attempt prematurely to confront and force her into ours. Although patients of the deflated narcissistic type may acquiesce to our confrontations and interpretations under the sway of the idealizing transference or the threat of losing us, they may only be repeating in the transference that surrender to an ambivalently idealized figure that traumatized them in the first place.

Likewise the overinflated narcissistic type, when prematurely confronted, may become enraged or even leave treatment, as this young woman considered doing. She, however, had been in treatment for some years and was on the verge of transition from insecurity to grandiosity in certain areas, a progressive movement for her. In this case her libidinal attachment to the therapist was sufficient to stand the strain of her ruptured narcissism, but if the same event had occurred two years earlier she might have left treatment without being able to understand why.

One may imagine that we are dealing here with an economic issue, constantly attempting to assess whether the weight of the patient's attachment will bear the strain of our interventions. And, indeed, this is nothing more than we ordinarily do in maintaining friendships and marriages, although to put it so bluntly might make it sound crass. But perhaps rather than only calculate whether, for example, our spouse's affections will tolerate yet another night away from home, what we also concurrently do is to put ourselves in the other's place and try to empathize with how our spouse might feel about it. And it seems we should always do this with our patients, for to treat them mechanically can only result in their reacting to us in a similar mechanical fashion.

All too many of our narcissistic patients have been brought up in mechanical ways. They have been socialized and trained to behave like human beings, but many feel inside as if they were only performing a ritual, going through the motions and, deep down, they know there is something wrong, something not real, something missing.

While many of these patients may indeed suffer from castration anxiety or penis envy, what they are also complaining of missing is an essential human quality, an inability to be in the world and to feel autonomous, self-sufficient, sexual, and alive. Ultimately, their complaints of inferiority, boredom, meaninglessness, and hypochondriasis refer to this feeling of emptiness that the deflated narcissist may express openly and that the overinflated narcissist defends against with counterphobic activity and manic denial. Although the grandiose narcissist seems to feel entitled to everything, whereas his deflated counterpart appears to feel entitled to nothing, deep down neither of them feels that he has a right to a life of his own. Indeed, many of our narcissistic patients do not feel a right to their own life, and certainly those with addictive problems like bulimics and anorectics do not feel a right even to their own bodies.

It may now become clearer why I place so much emphasis on the narcissistic patient emotionally owning his treatment, because for someone who may not feel a right even to his own life or his own body, it will be a constant problem to feel that he has a right to his own treatment.

As you may anticipate, the issue goes far deeper than finding a benevolent therapist who will permit the patient to have a voice in his treatment. By the time we see such patients, intricate defensive operations have evolved so that they are no longer capable or even desirous of collaborating in their treatment. Instead, the deflated narcissist wants *you* to control him so that he becomes your slave and is empowered by you, and the grandiose narcissist wants to control *you* so that you become his slave and are unable to help him. This plunges us squarely into problems of sadomasochism.

It should not be surprising to discover that sadomasochism is so ubiquitous in the narcissistic disorders since I have already suggested that a frequent fixation point is in the anal/depressive/ rapprochement/bisexual phase. We are all familiar with both the clinging and the sadistic aspects of anality and rapprochement and the alternating omnipotence and helplessness characteristic of this age.

It is at this time that the toddler is beginning to integrate his sense of wholeness and aliveness (*subjective awareness*) with his parents' and his own developing perspective on himself as one person among many others (*objective self-awareness*). It is also at this time that he is struggling to integrate the extremes of overinflated and deflated self-representations and object representations. Externally, one sees this in the clinging and sadistic behavior that has made this period known as the "terrible twos." When this struggle to develop evocative constancy and to modulate and regulate the self- and object representations does not go well, then the representational stage is already set for the child to slip easily into the mode of sadomasochism.

Indeed, we might see this stage as a decisive preoedipal influence on the future love life of the child. We have noted that the normal or neurotic can experience both himself and his objects as cohesive and alive because in normal development the self and object representations develop simultaneously and self-love develops concurrently with object love. In the narcissistic disorders, however, this process seems to have gone awry.

The overinflated narcissist denigrates his objects yet needs them to love him, while the deflated narcissist idealizes his objects, who repeatedly disillusion him. These distortions of the love life arise because self love and object love have not developed interdependently, and this lack of reciprocity gives them a pathological distortion.

Let me take as an example the case of a mother who lacked self-esteem and masochistically allowed herself to be denigrated by her husband. She then endowed her baby son with her lost phallic-narcissistic powers and he grew up to be an overinflated narcissist, denigrating the very mother who admired him. In this case one might say that the growth of the child's object love for his mother had not kept pace with the growth of his self-love leading to a pathological imbalance in favor of a distorted self-love.

Another example is the case of a very self-centered mother whose narcissism, for complicated reasons, did not extend to her daughter. Unrecognized and unsupported by her mother, this little girl turned to idealizing her father in order to stay alive. In later life she becomes a deflated narcissistic type, feeling inferior and insecure, always looking to worship a powerful man who would protect her. In this case one might say that the growth of the little girl's self-love had not kept pace with the growth of her object love, with a pathological imbalance favoring a distorted object love.

When this struggle to modulate self and object representations and to develop evocative constancy does not go well, the child is constantly faced with insoluble either-or dilemmas. He cannot arrive at a point that will allow him multiple perspectives on the events in his world, nor a vision that will even slightly legitimize both his view and the view of others. Thus each interaction becomes a battle over the preservation of his very existence, a struggle to the death, a sadomasochistic encounter.

We find that the sadomasochistic attitude runs like a red thread through all the narcissistic disorders: not only the sexual perversions but also the addictions, the eating disorders, and the psychosomatic disorders, as well as the more common character disorders. Alternations between sadism and masochism are ubiquitous and they parallel and reflect fluctuations in self-inflation and self-depletion, in objective and subjective self-awareness and in self-regulation.

I would not want to leave you with the impression that sadomasochism is uniquely an issue of self-representations and self-regulation, for we know that it also involves fascinating problems of pleasure in pain, sexualization of aggression, anal fixations, and issues of autonomy. Normal relationships are loosely coupled systems that leave room for each partner's autonomy, but narcissistic and sadomasochistic relationships are tightly coupled systems which, as we shall see in the next chapter, leave little space for individual autonomy. Such relationships are totally entwined, controlling and controlled which is one reason they are often of unusual intensity but also tend to burn out rather rapidly.

Although most patients with narcissistic and borderline transferences will show sadomasochistic fantasies, only some will show actual sexual perversions. While all these patients have undifferentiated self- and object representations, the development of an actual perversion seems to require some particular elision of the relationship to reality.

I have suggested in the previous chapter that many sadomasochistic relationships are connected to some early loss that has not been mourned, so that sado-masochistic fluctuations may be viewed as a kind of pathological mourning, a frantic oscillation between admitting that the object is lost or dead and asserting that it is still alive and available. But this, too, can be seen as a problem of object constancy, although there are always elements of defense and compromise formation as well. Our concern is how to deal with the sadomasochistic transference and countertransference that will inevitably arise when we work with these patients.

I feel that our attitude in beginning the treatment may be crucial in this respect, and I have mentioned how important it is for the patient to experience the treatment as a collaborative endeavor rather than as the analyst's exclusive province. While a true collaboration may be something that the patient has never before experienced in either his work, his relationships, or his previous therapies, we should nevertheless endeavor to achieve this throughout the vicissitudes of a transference that may run the gamut from mildly to profoundly sadomasochistic. And in order to achieve this goal with patients whose symptoms are grandiosity, idealization, disparagement, and denial, we can do no better than to learn to deal with our own parallel feelings, which will constantly be aroused in our ongoing struggles with the inevitable narcissistic countertransference.

CHAPTER 3

The Language of Perversion and the Language of Love

A NUMBER OF YEARS ago I had occasion to observe a young woman who was intensely engaged in a thrilling but frightening affair with a bisexual man who wore her clothing during sex. This cross-dressing was not simply an eccentric preference but was characteristic of the entire relationship, which was based on confused identifications and their use of each other as part-objects in a shared fantasy of the phallic woman. After years of analysis in the course of which the woman left this man and found someone she loved, she was able to observe: "Mark's penis was a fascinating object unto itself, whereas Richard's penis is simply a part of him and it's wonderful because it's his." I made a mental note that she had switched from the language of perversion to the language of love.

I was also interested to observe that the phallic woman fantasies and beating fantasies that had loomed so large in the perverse relationship had not entirely disappeared from analytic view, but had rather become transformed in the course of the patient's change of character. Upon reflection, this did not seem so strange because, although most analysts agree that the beating fantasy (Freud 1919, Novick and Novick 1987) and the phallic woman fantasy (Bak 1968) are essential elements of the perversions, these fantasies arise in the course of normal development and might therefore also be found in the normal adult. It seemed that one of the distinctions between normality and perversion must lie not in the presence or absence of these particular fantasies nor even in their degree of activity or of consciousness, but rather in the level at which they were organized and integrated in the psychic structure.

It is worth noting that both these fantasies involve paradoxes. The phallic woman fantasy is a fantasy about a woman with male genitals, that is, a bisexual paradox embodying the question: is she male or female or both? The beating fantasy is a fantasy about being mistreated by someone as a sign that he loves you, that is, an ambivalent paradox embodying the question: does he love me or hate me or both?

A paradox is a seemingly contradictory statement that may nevertheless be true. There is at least one paradox with which we all struggle as a developmental fact and that we all resolve or fail to resolve in ways that profoundly affect our character. I mean the paradox that we are born as part of another human being but are also separate and must eventually become our own human being. I believe it is this paradox about how we can be both united with someone and separate from that person that underlies the paradoxical questions of perversion. A corollary paradox is how we can both live in this world and yet remain separate from it, that is, how we can subjectively experience our unique internal world and yet also look at ourselves objectively as a person among other persons, a thing among things. These corollary paradoxes, of being both united and separate, of being both in the world and out of it, form the matrix on which our identity is built.

I have deliberately widened the issue of perversion from one of sexual identity to one of identity in general in order to include character perversions and also perverse relationships, where the other person is used as a functional or part-object. Perversion in this larger sense is a lack of capacity for whole-object love. While both sorts of perversions seem to have similar structure and dynamics, perverse relationships need not include overt sexual perversions such as fetishism, transvestism, or exhibitionism. But it is my impression that most sexual perversions do seem to involve part-object relationships and thus deal with issues far wider than whether the woman does or does not have a penis, although that *is* a very important question indeed.

When Freud noted that perverts puzzle about the answer to this question and appear both to know it and not know it at the same time, he postulated a vertical split in the ego, a concept with widening implications. For we have all been in situations where we find ourselves both believing and disbelieving something at the same time. In the midst of a traumatic accident, for example, it is common to feel "I can't believe this is happening to me!" But we generally *behave* as if it *were* happening, whereas the pervert seems to behave as if he both believed *and* disbelieved it. It is conceivable that at some level we all still believe and disbelieve that women have penises for we may all have believed it at one time, but the pervert is someone who continues to *enact* this belief and disbelief. We may well wonder why the pervert keeps obsessively raising and reenacting a question that the rest of us have, if not settled, at least exiled to another part of our psyche. At first blush one might think we have relegated it to the unconscious, but we then realize that the phallic woman fantasy may be conscious or unconscious for both perverts and normals. If this is true, why is it constantly being questioned and reenacted only with the pervert?

It would seem that perversion involves not only a fantasy and its status in consciousness but also important issues of mental structure and reality relationship as well. Those of us who live normally with the phallic-woman fantasy have presumably indexed it as a fantasy and have accepted the actual sexual differences as real. The classical sexual pervert, on the other hand, has never accepted the reality of the two sexes or of the vagina and he uses avowal and disavowal of the phallus to perpetuate a unisex fantasy of "everybody's got it but now you see it and now you don't."

Those of us who live normally with the phallic-woman fantasy have managed to deal with it in some transitional space, through play, mythology, jokes, and artistic creation, for in the reality of our behavior we have settled the matter. But people with perverse relationships seem to lack this transitional space, leaving them excessively preoccupied with concrete answers to the paradoxes of life.

To live comfortably with the paradoxes of bisexuality or ambivalence one must first have the ability to hold a paradoxical idea in mind without eliminating one side or the other. As we watch young children grope to categorize self and other, male and female, living and dead, we come to recognize that while the dichotomous categorization is a developmental achievement, it is often too arbitrary to adequately encompass all of human experience.

A toddler first learning to differentiate *mine* from *yours* may often carry this process to its ultimate antagonistic extreme; only much later will he be able to grasp the concept of *ours*. Likewise, it is a developmental achievement for children to learn they may have two desires that are equally reasonable but cannot both be fulfilled because they conflict with each other. It is even more difficult to understand that the same reality can be viewed in different ways by different people and that both points of view can be equally justifiable. Of course, some children never do fully develop these capacities, and we also find adults who never developed these capacities or have functionally lost them.

Among this latter group we find Freud's (1915) "women of elemental passionateness who tolerate no surrogates," who are "amenable only to the logic of soup with dumplings for arguments" (pp. 166–167). These women, and men also, mistake transference love for the "real thing" and demand consummation because they are unable to deal with metaphor or to tolerate the idea that they and their analyst may have two very different points of view on the same reality. Today we might view this "elemental passionateness" as a perversion of love, since it is a love that is not returned and that refuses to recognize the real existence or real desires of the beloved object.

In sum, we might say that one of the characteristics of perversion is a difficulty in dealing with metaphor and multiple points of view and in tolerating ambiguous or paradoxical situations. Instead of multiple points of view we find splitting, and instead of tolerance for ambiguity and paradox we find either-or alternatives. These disorders of thinking are *the cognitive aspect of representational disorders,* that is, disorders of self and object representations and self and object constancy. Let me try to clarify this with a clinical example.

Arnold was a man with a wildly intrusive psychotic mother, who in his twenties had found the strength to leave home and never to see her again. But in his thirties he developed an obsessive passion for a Spanish girl he met while she was vacationing in this country. In bed, Arnold would sensually feed this "sweet young girl," then perform cunnilingus and then lick her clean. She passively allowed him to do whatever he wished. But when she returned to Spain he became desperate, followed her there, was obsessed with the idea of losing her and found himself on the roof of a building about to jump. He would willingly have given up his life and his business in this country to be with her, but she professed only friendship. He developed severe insomnia, bulimia, and suicidal ideation. Treatment[1] began in a halting manner since he fought every attempt at commitment for more than a week at a time. It was characteristic that he should be totally obsessed with seeing this woman who did *not* wish to see him, while staving off every attempt at contact by the therapist who did wish to see him. He could vacillate only between total dependence and total independence. Gradually he calmed down, but the enactment in the transference continued to replay his attempts at both relating to and fending off his psychotic mother.

As a teenager he rode his motorcycle to escape from his fear of maternal engulfment; later he became a pilot and a hang-glider. When he eventually moved into analysis he had no reactions to the analyst's vacations but took up sky diving instead. He was constantly manipulating the frequency of sessions and using extra-transferential figures in order to avoid a fantasied engulfment in the transference, an engulfment he both longed for and feared. He was afraid of losing himself in the transference and developing an obsession with the analyst as he had with the Spanish girl. He was able to say: "When I think of myself, when I'm into myself, like in flying or sky diving, then I forget about you, but when I think about you, then I forget about myself!" But while all the flying and diving enactments were both a fleeing from the mother and an assertion of self-sufficiency, they also concealed the wish to fall back into mother earth and be lovingly clasped to her breast.

---

[1]This exemplary treatment was conducted by Miriam Pierce, C.S.W., to whom I am indebted for this material.

This fantasy of return to the womb is reenacted with the Spanish girl when he feeds her lovingly, then eats her when she is fattened up, and licks the platter clean. But the necessary condition to avoid his own fear of being eaten is that she remain absolutely passive; she complies, she submits and she makes no demands. Either she is the "sweet young girl" or else she becomes the dangerous phallic woman. He cannot conceive of her as a "sweet young girl" who might also have desires of her own.

In the second year of treatment Arnold returned from summer vacation still talking of reducing the frequency of sessions and not wanting to keep the analyst in mind lest she take him over, but he related that he had met a woman who interested him and he was thinking of living with her. He noted that problems arose with Annie similar to those with the analyst: would she trap him? should he be forced into monogamy? By the middle of the year some of this had been worked through and he rented a house with Annie, but only for a renewable one-year lease, as he renewed the analysis each year.

He had a dream about some sort of wedding ceremony. "I was watching this from a wall, a circular wall. I was sitting on top of the wall and it was about forty feet down to the floor. There was a wedding party down there, in this circle. Annie was with me. I was aware that it was dangerous to be watching from this wall and there was a long fall to the floor. There was also a floor behind me that was also far, if we were to fall, but not as far as the one in front. I remember thinking that it was too crowded down there in the circle, but the wall was comfortable because it was a wide wall and you could sit on it and just watch."

Arnold's first association was to a wedding ring and how confining that would be for him . . . he was sitting on the fence with regard to marriage. The long fall forward for this sky-diver would be a commitment to marriage and a potential reengulfment with the psychotic mother, but the fall backwards would be the break-up with Annie and a depression like the one he had gone through with the Spanish girl. One thing was very different, however; he was now sitting on the wall together with Annie and it was a comfortable space—"it was a wide wall and you could sit on it and just watch."

The feeling at this time, that we were witnessing the creation of a transitional space, was borne out in the course of subsequent events. By the following summer he was able to come in after the vacation, sit facing the analyst, and talk about the difficulties of missing her and the changes that had occurred in each. For the first time since the treatment began both he and the analyst could comfortably occupy the same space at the same time without danger or fear for either one.

Let me now contrast the fantasy in this "dream of the wide wall" with some fantasies of the Marquis de Sade, written while he was imprisoned in the Bastille:

"He has himself frigged by his lackey while the girl, naked, balances upon a narrow pedestal; all the while he is being frigged, she may neither budge nor lose her equilibrium" (1966, p. 587).

Or again:

"He makes her sit down in an armchair balanced on springs. . . . Certain levers and gears advance twenty daggers until their points graze her skin; the man frigs himself, the while explaining that the least movement of the chair will cause her to be stabbed. . . . " (1966, p. 609).

Here we have a universe that is terrifying precisely because it contains no free or transitional space—every impingement of one being upon the other, every assertion by the object of its separateness or individuality becomes a matter of life and death. It is probably no coincidence that the inventor of this sadomasochistic universe had, like Arnold, suffered a traumatic early separation from his mother. One might view these fantasies as a desperately failing attempt to rework and compensate this trauma, an insane endeavor to isolate and encapsulate the anguish in frozen space and time.

How is it that an open or transitional space develops, free from the impingements that Arnold experienced or that the Marquis de Sade was obliged to re-create again and again? I describe in Chapter 5 how in the good-enough mother–infant equilibrium a space evolves, free from the impingements of external or internal stimuli, within which the infant can begin to consolidate his own autonomy. This interactional exchange is repeated, mutually reorganized and reintegrated at higher levels at each developmental stage.

Arnold's psychotic mother was never able to establish an adequate equilibrium with him from the earliest days to the day of his leaving. His mother's intrusiveness can be metaphorically pictured as the intrusiveness of a mother who never allows the baby to avoid her gaze but is constantly pursuing him while he tries to escape, a form of interaction that has been named "chase and dodge" (Beebe and Stern 1977). So Arnold grew up dodging, and when he eventually became mobile he left the scene completely.

His history was the history of a child who at each developmental phase was unconsciously searching for the appropriate interactional experience he had missed, a search I describe in Chapter 6. This search finally came to rest in his analysis where the analyst, through holding, reenactment, and interpretation, allowed this longed-for equilibrium to develop in the analytic system. In the relationship with Annie we see these mutual interactions being laboriously worked through, reorganized, and transformed and a transitional space finally emerging in the dream of the wide wall.

But before such therapeutic transformations occur, the mind in perversion remains structured in terms of either-or alternatives and their corresponding mental splits, with little capacity to recognize multiple points of view or to deal with metaphor and paradox. This makes therapeutic work in the transference difficult or impossible until a space has been established that allows the two parties to at least coexist in the same place at the same time. Let me give another example:

> Kent, a young man who had great difficulty in both his work and his sexual relationships, entered analysis after several previously failed attempts. As the transference deepened, it became more and more unbearable for him to hear me speak, no matter what I said or how I said it. It seemed clear that this was a transference reaction to an intolerably intrusive psychotic parent, but though I interpreted this in many ways and although Kent at times could see my point, there was a part of him that was able to treat the situation only as a concrete reality. Since the treatment seemed about to fail just as the previous treatments had, I finally decided to hold my peace and say not a word more. During all this time Kent continued to attend religiously; he lay on the couch, free associated, and interpreted his own dreams, associations, and behavior, including some transference reactions. Once or twice during that time I tried to utter a word but was met with such protest and a week-long disruption that I had little choice but to remain silent.
>
> After a very long time, shortly before the summer break, he reported a dream in which he had killed his best friend and awakened in panic, horrified that they could no longer play together.
>
> I said: "That sounds like what you're afraid might happen between you and me."
>
> He then explained with some wonderment, as if we had been talking all along, that when I spoke he would have to give up his own thinking and concentrate on what I was thinking. He would lose himself entirely—he would be dead. That's why whatever I said was like torture to him— either he would be murdered or I would be murdered.

Now I was going away for the summer and he was guilty because he was afraid he had killed me and he couldn't be sure that I would ever come back. But something seemed to have happened . . . we had begun to talk together and perhaps that might continue should we meet again in the fall.

Indeed something had happened: a psychic space had been opened in which impingements were not mutually destructive but that, like the wide wall in Arnold's dream, was a comfortable place where you could just sit with someone and watch. Just as Arnold's actions in fleeing from his mother were self-defining and boundary forming, just as his enactments in the transference served to strengthen and clarify the limits of self and other until they could coexist without danger, so Kent's silencing of me served the purpose of humbling me and defining his own power and my boundaries. It might be fair to call this a *mutual enactment in the transference*: he of his fear and hatred of his father and his loving determination to force me to become a good-enough parent; me of my rage at his behavior and my despair at ever being able to help him. Once passed through, we could meet as coequals in the no-man's-land of a transference that was not unilaterally owned or pathologized by either one of us but was a space for shared fantasies and playing.

Although it may take much patience and a very long time to achieve such a psychic space, once it has opened the treatment seems to progress rather rapidly. Perhaps this is partly because it has moved from a one-person to a two-person psychology and the parameters have become very different; for example learning from the other person is now a possibility. But the fundamental reason is that some basic mutual trust has developed, an analytic trust (Ellman 1991) forged in the smithy of the transference, something that with these patients could never be achieved by words alone. Perhaps here I may be permitted an aside.

For the longest time in psychoanalysis action was viewed with a kind of mistrust: the patient was cautioned never to take important actions during analysis, his every act was viewed as an acting-out of what should be verbalized, and the analyst himself was expected to abjure any action that might reveal himself or his motivations. The history of this repudiation of action no doubt begins with Breuer's first fright at what the transference had wrought and continues through Freud's famous dispute with Ferenczi about his grand experiments. But with our growing understanding that no action is also an action and that acting-out in both the transference and the countertransference is to some degree inevitable, some reevaluation of this has been taking place (Boesky 1982, Chused 1991, Jacobs 1986, McLaughlin 1991).

Certainly when we work with the perversions, addictions, and borderline and narcissistic personalities, it seems clear that enactments are sometimes the only form of authentic communication the patient is able to make. And sometimes the analyst must meet such enactments with the only form of communication the patient can hear, which may not be an an interpretation of its meaning but rather a containment or even a counterenactment by the analyst. For we are dealing here with a group of people who, like Freud's "soup and dumpling" patients, have for good reason lost their faith in words, and for them we must reestablish the basis of trust in reality that resides in action and its consequences.

For Kent, my words invaded his ego space and murdered him; for Arnold, his therapist's words made him forget himself and remember only her. Another patient told me that she couldn't allow me to come alive in the hour because if I came alive I might get up and leave her, a more sublimated version of Sade's fantasies of immobilizing his love object. For such patients we must facilitate the creation of a safe transitional space, safe because we do not engage in seductive or destructive violations of their boundaries, but a space in which play action can take place, just as I was "playing dead" for Kent.

It seems that transitional space occupies a privileged position in the psyche, much as in the Middle Ages the church steps provided asylum from secular authorities. One might see it as an indispensable refuge from the strain of ongoing conflict and the harsh realities of life. But whereas a politically neutral space is a given for everyone, transitional space cannot be "given" to someone because it requires an active taking or "making" on the part of the patient, a creative act. In this view an act on the part of some patients, whether it be an enactment, a transference acting-out, or a reaction against the analytic framework, always carries the potential for being a creative act if it is met by a creative analytic response. And granted that we cannot all be masters of the Squiggle game, at the very least we can avoid immobilizing our objects and compressing transitional space like Sade.

This kind of enactment in the transference is comprised of an original action by the patient that is met by a creative response from the analyst. It is always initiated by the patient and springs from a trust that allows the patient to make the first move. I remember early in my career a disturbed young woman who appeared one day carrying an extremely large and heavy oil painting of her father. When I hesitated to accept it and inquired about her reason for bringing it, she threw it out the open window where it narrowly missed injuring a passerby seven stories below. Her creative action in bringing me the portrait to protect her father while she talked about him was met by my stupidity, evoking instantaneous rage and despair. From this I learned that the world of classical analytic "technique" and the world of play had different rules, and that the latter had not yet been codified. We are making a beginning in comprehending the world of play, as Steingart (in press) points out, when we understand that experiences are probably encoded in two ways, both in action and in words, both pictorially and linguistically (Freud 1900) both by analogue encoding and by digital encoding (Bucci 1985, 1989). But it also became clear to me that the rules of analytic technique, while generally the best guide we can offer, may on occasion be perverted to anyone's purpose.

It might be interesting to compare an act of perversion with an act of play to see if we can distinguish some of the differences. Let me take as text one of the milder episodes in Sade cited earlier:

"He has himself frigged by his lackey while the girl, naked, balances upon a narrow pedestal; all the while he is being frigged, she may neither budge nor lose her equilibrium" (1966, p. 609).

We note immediately how the object is allowed no space at all to act freely, that is, she may not budge upon pain of death. Most perversions, of course, do not have an implied death threat, but the ultimate threat for noncompliance is always separation and loss. We can also notice the enormous emphasis on the *inequality* between the man and his object: she is naked, he is not; she is helpless, he is in control; she is alone, he has a lackey; she is required neither to budge nor to lose her equilibrium, he is free to act in any way he wants and especially to lose his equilibrium in orgasm. She seems to be reduced to nothing, a mere object to mirror his grandiosity, yet we know that she is the projection of an essential part of his psyche and were she to be gone his sadomasochistic world would disappear and his sadism turn to suicide (Bach and Schwartz 1972).

Here we have an either-or world view where everything rejected in oneself is projected onto the other who no longer exists as an object in herself but merely as a carrier for the not-me. Sade's fear for the loss of his own equilibrium is concretized in the mad balancing act, a world where the slightest misstep can lead to annihilation. The mere notion that the object might have a point of view is unthinkable; likewise, it is inadmissable that any act might mean other than what it *is*. The act has been totally decontextualized and desymbolized; shorn of all moral, cultural, and personal connections so that it is deprived of everything that might give it meaning. The language is concise, efficient, and mechanically depersonalized, the same language one might use to call down artillery fire or order the execution of hostages. This is military language applied to human relationships, the language of perversion.

Let us contrast this with an act of play with which we are all perfectly familiar, the interplay between parent and child. Here the baby is allowed maximum space to act freely and, although the threat of separation and loss is still present, it is playfully handled through ritualized games such as Peek-a-Boo and This Little Piggy. Here the glaring inequality between the participants is artfully minimized, and who is big and who is little and who has power and who has not is either irrelevant or a subject of mirth. Indeed, even body parts may be playfully exchanged: I've got your nose! Whose eyes are these? Now it's mine and now it's yours—just as in the interplay between lovers, body parts may be exchanged and interchanged, including genitalia.

Typically, the parent and baby at play will not be concerned about loss of equilibrium; rather, there will be an interactive mutual and self-regulation so that each will accelerate or brake the other, allowing time for both solos and ensemble, like a good jazz group (Stern 1985). Neither participant is merely a mirror for the other nor entirely dependent on the other; each has a world of his own that must be allowed for and respected.

Rather than a field in which fantasies are unilaterally projected, here we have a field in which fantasies are mutually shared and enjoyed; where there can be no such thing as a misstep because the desire is to accommodate completely. Rather than annihilating the other's point of view as in Sade, the baby is *endowed* with a point of view, and a meaning is *attributed* to his every action so that he becomes enmeshed in a network of symbolism that gives meaning to his life. Indeed, parents begin to create a context of meaning for each baby, sometimes even before the child is conceived, and the normal baby becomes the nexus of a web of extended social, cultural, and personal meanings and fantasies.

These shared fantasies are one hallmark of an act of play, just as the unilaterally imposed fantasy is the hallmark of an act of violence. Perversions fall somewhere in between, but perverse fantasies have a distinctive relationship to reality. We have seen how baby and parent can play at exchanging body parts in the transitional area—I've got your nose; whose fingers are these?—just as lovers may play at exchanging genitalia.

But this play requires an absolute trust between the partners, which is lacking in the perversions.

The perverse fantasy exchange always remains too close to the kernel of trauma within each perverse fantasy and thus too close to the possibility of betrayal. It is always in danger of really coming true and producing terror, whereas the play fantasy relies on mutual trust. It may be that it is precisely this act of working together in an atmosphere of trust to produce a mutually acceptable fantasy and a mutually acceptable tension state that characterizes the act of play.

In a way, one might consider the perversion as a repeatedly failed attempt to create a transitional space, but though it is often presented in a playful way it is really a form of pseudo-play. For instead of playfully exchanging body parts as do lovers or mother and child, the pervert forcefully attempts to create a unilateral change *in reality*. His fragile ego and unstable representational world cannot permit the moratorium on reality testing necessary for a playful exchange to take place in transitional space. For him the question of "does she or doesn't she" remains on the concrete level and is thus a deadly serious business. Indeed, if we look to the psychotic we can see that the alternation between knowing and not knowing has entirely disappeared; the exchange of body parts has becomes even more literal and has actually taken place. Schreber is convinced that he has irreversibly become a woman and that he has the body parts to prove it.

It appears that when we analyze such primal fantasies as phallic woman or beating fantasies we do not eliminate but rather transform them. They become utilizeable at different levels, and it is the organization within which the fantasy operates that determines whether it symbolically enriches our psyche through art, mythology, and loving playfulness, or whether it concretely destroys us through lifeless and meaningless perverse acts or self-destruction and mutilation.

Thus it is not the fantasy itself that is pathological; these are developmentally based fantasies that are ubiquitous in illness *and* in health. What is pathological in perverse relationships is the undifferentiated and unstable object world existing in a psychic space unable to contain separate autonomous objects.

Likewise, it is not the fantasies that are abolished in a therapeutic cure but the self- and object representations that are raised to higher levels of differentiation, interaction, and constancy. As the conflicts around dependency, separation, and aggression diminish, more mature self-representations can flexibly accommodate both subjective and objective self-awareness, so that the patient is able not only to live in his experience, but is also able to observe himself and reflect on his behavior. This growing self-awareness allows for a level of symbolic functioning that can accommodate both archaic and sublimated versions of the fantasy and can handle both metaphor and paradox.

In practicing psychoanalysis with the more disturbed patients, we work to create a transitional space within which the transference can be experienced both as a living reality and can also be seen as a metaphor. This is the lesson of Freud's "soup and dumplings" patients who were considered untreatable at that time. In cases where we succeed in doing this, the patient begins to understand in a rich and emotional way that *the same reality can be viewed in different ways by different people, and that his point of view and the analyst's point of view can both have reality and legitimacy.*

Often it is only after arriving at this point that interpretations of libidinal and aggressive conflicts become useable and mutative.

Thus I am suggesting that phallic woman and beating fantasies are universal but that the pervert is obliged to reenact them in a concrete way, whereas normals are able to deal with them through symbolic transformations in the transitional area. The ability to deal with primal fantasies via transformations begins in childhood in the potential space between inner life and outer reality, and it begins with mutual acceptance of the paradoxes of internal and external, mind and body, and two in one. Gradually an ego capacity develops for the tolerance and transformation of paradoxes that cannot be resolved, a language of creative ego functioning.

For the pervert, on the other hand, this transitional space and creative ego capacity has been blocked or undeveloped, and it should be a major objective in treating people with perversions not to condemn their inevitable acting-out, but to change these concrete reenactments into symbolic transformations through the provision of an ego space that contains them.

Thus, while the language of normal creativity is the language of serious paradox accepted, understood, and grappled with as we grapple, for example, with our bisexuality through the fantasy of the phallic woman, so the language of perversion is a language of paradox refused and reduced to an either-or choice that is handled through splitting, projection, and reenactments. I believe it is a worthwhile task for the analyst to see himself as a translator, working to help transform the language of perversion into the language of normal human paradox, that is, the language of love.

CHAPTER 4

The Elusive Image

FROM ANCIENT EGYPTIAN times until the present, children have always played seeking games (Opie and Opie 1969), that is, games in which one or a group of children hide while another child, who is deliberately disoriented by being blindfolded, twirled, or otherwise confused, is then obliged to search for the missing players. Great is the excitement at finding or being found, and this thrill and exhilaration holds across all the developmental levels (Peller 1954) from the infant's joy at playing Peek-a-Boo (Kleeman 1967), through the oedipal and latency games of I Spy and Hide and Go Seek, to our latest technologized versions where adults seeking mates sort through thousands of computerized photos, hoping to find the image that echoes their imagination.

While this might seem a far cry from Dante's first glimpse of Beatrice or Petrarch's of Laura, the theme of seeking and finding a known or unknown face and the subsequent shock or thrill of recognition has permeated art, mythology, and literature through the millennia, summed up in the popular hope that on some enchanted evening we will meet the stranger we long for.

One might well wonder what it is that all these

seekers, from Arthur in the *Faerie Queen* to Dracula, who was also seeking his beloved, have been looking for. I would like to differentiate this search for an elusive image from the Quest theme, where the object is something of value like the Holy Grail, the quest for which must be pursued by heroic deeds against all odds but that, when captured, confers everlasting glory, power, or triumph of some sort.

By contrast, the search for an image, a vision, is always mysterious, ambiguous, and elusive because, unlike the Holy Grail, it is not an object that can be permanently captured. Besides, even when the elusive image is apprehended, it may not necessarily be spiritually uplifting or beautiful; in the shock of recognition it may indeed turn out to be rejecting, frightening, or repulsive: La Belle Dame sans Merci or the Medusa's head.

To a greater or lesser extent we all pursue visions, hoping to find in the material world a match for the images of our psychic reality. It was Freud, of course, who first noted that the finding of an object is always a refinding (1905), always, that is, a search for the parental or sibling imagoes, whether current, past or wished-for. And it was again Freud who noted that in certain cases the imago may also be a vision of the self (1914), either the current self, the past self, or a wished-for self.

But it was only under the influence of work with very disturbed patients and of recent infant research that we have begun to fully appreciate the extent to which the earliest mutual interactions underlie our most primitive imagoes and indeed the very substrate of our ego functions. In particular, work with acting-out and addictive patients as well as research in self and mutual regulation and mutual gazing have taught us a great deal about problems in the development of evocative self and object constancy.

I mean by evocative object constancy the ability to emotionally recall an object in its absence and to experience it as a vital living presence, and by evocative self constancy, the ability to hold on to a vital and coherent image of oneself in the absence of a supporting or confirming object. I believe that evocative self and object constancy are the cornerstones of both the symbolizing process and the capacity to feel like oneself in an ongoing way.

To be ongoing means to be able to link the past, the present, and the future in such a way as to feel actively alive in time and space. When parents notice their children's unique capacities and envisage how they might use them as adults, they are making them a gift of the future, and when they review with their toddler what has gone on during the day or retell "how we took that trip last year," they are making them a gift of the past. This linking of the past, present, and future contributes to a sense of history and destiny that makes one feel alive in the stream of time.

The symbolizing process also involves a linkage and integration, not only of different realms of time but of different domains and functions of the mind such as conscious and unconscious, primary and secondary process, and nonverbal and verbal or enactive and lexical processes of encoding (Bucci 1985, 1989; Steingart in press); an integration of parts of the self (Loewald 1978). There are many patients who have not yet established a secure sense of ongoingness in time and space, and in them the symbolizing process is also insecure or defective. Those who do not have firmly established self-constancy are forever seeking a confirming object, while those whose object constancy is not secure may pursue idealized objects as if seeking to recover the links of a chain that have broken and scattered.

What I am talking about here, then, is not the search that Freud described for the imago of the loving or unloving object mother, but rather the search for the mothering functions before they have become linked and integrated as part of a whole human being. This is Winnicott's (1965) environmental mother, whose ministrations form the very fabric of our ego structure, our sense of aliveness, of ongoingness in time and space and of self-constancy. It is this early functional mother of environment, before her full recognition as a whole object, whose recurrent touch and caring awakens the infant's sensual being to a love of its own body and a certainty of its libidinal existence. And it is this same mother of libidinization who, by her consistent attunement, endows the infant with a dependable sense of I AM and a sense of self-constancy.

Thus, the search that I am describing is not for the image of the object mother nor for a self-image, past or wished-for. It is rather *the search for a function or series of functions,* including the libidinizing and constancy functions, the carrier of which may appear under the guise of a maternal object or under some other guise. And just as Anna Freud (1967) describes children who have lost their object mother or been lost by her as constantly losing things, so children who have lost their environmental mothering functions are constantly tending not only to lose things but to lose their own sense of well being, their sense of orientation in the world, and even their sense of themselves.

The most striking examples of this that come to mind are the addictions, for in this view an addiction is in part a lifelong quest to artificially replace a basic regulatory function that was lacking or inadequately supplied by the environment. The reasons for this inadequacy may be complex—social or political as well as psychological, always including the possibility that the child himself was so deviant or ill that he couldn't utilize what was offered. But whatever the cause, addicts of food and drugs are the clearest examples of those who search for a regulatory imago; clearest because in these cases the imago happens to *be* a thing rather than a love object *used* as a function or thing.

The Aztecs and the Indians called their sacred intoxicants "God's flesh" and "God's messenger," and a contemporary patient who used heroin on a regular basis called it "God's hug." Certain anorectics use starvation for religious-libidinal purposes, while some bulimics eat particular foods that make them feel more masculine or more feminine. As we watch both food and drug addicts in their struggles with the addictive substance, it becomes clear that they are attempting to regulate their space, their constancy, their degree of libidinization, and their emotions by interacting with the substance as if it were the good/bad environmental mother they are missing. In analysis, they progress from this concrete functional use of the good/bad substance to a concrete functional use of the good/bad analyst as provider of environment and then to a view of the analyst as a good and bad whole object.

Indeed, it is because the provision of function is so important for these patients, preferably 24 hours a day, that adjuvant treatment such as Twelve Step programs or hospitals are often necessary to cover the management involved. Of course, the severe addictions and eating and psychosomatic disorders are at a lower developmental level than the narcissistic disorders and perversions with which I am primarily concerned here.

While the narcissistic and perverse disorders may show addictive, bulorectic, and psychosomatic tendencies, these are milder and have been "dragged along," as it were, from the earlier level of development. The narcissistic and perverse patient has benefited from an early narcissistic relationship with the mother and is libidinized and possesses a symbolic object, even if the mother sees only herself in the child. But when the mother does not "see" the child at all then libidinization and symbolization may be profoundly arrested, and it is in these more severe disorders that we find decathexis, asymbolia, and alexithymia.

While with drug or food addicts it is abundantly clear that they search for the environmental "mother" who will provide the regulatory functions they need to stay alive, the issues become much more subtle with better adjusted patients. For example, it is part of the psychopathology of everyday life that women who as children found their mothers lacking in certain maternal capacities when they went shopping together compensate for this as adults by going shopping with another woman who fulfills these missing functions.

Let me begin by illustrating this view with some ordinary clinical examples:

Peter was a brilliant young lawyer who came to therapy because of difficulties with relationships. Although in his mid-thirties and functioning at a high level of proficiency, he had had only one relationship; a disastrous affair with a bisexual man who worked in the post office and whom Peter idealized for his beauty.

Peter was the only child of a foreign-born couple who both seemed somewhat schizoid. Throughout his childhood the three of them would sit around in different rooms watching three different television sets tuned to three different stations. When he first came to therapy he lived in a split-off narcissistic world that he managed to conceal from everyone by his charm, intelligence, and intense efforts to behave as people would expect him to. But in his private state, which he referred to as "Peter's world" and which he kept hidden even from his lover, he had grandiose fantasies that he was a godlike figure, read esoteric literature, worked on obscure stories, and kept a secret diary. In the course of therapy he began to try to make a real relationship with a real person, but he was often at a loss about how to proceed.

One weekend he attended a convention in another part of the country and was disturbed when his senior partner seemed to ignore him in the hall. He worried that this nonrecognition portended dismissal from his job, a kind of paranoid reaction that had often appeared in the transference and that seemed to mean: *Recognize me for something, even if it's bad!* He said:

"Even when I'm in a group I feel solitary. Last week I was reading Kerouac's *On the Road* and now I'm reading this biography of him. I feel more connected to Kerouac than to the people I work with, or even to Martin (his lover). Kerouac was writing about his old friend Cassidy, and in order to understand him better Kerouac tried to repeat everything that Cassidy had done. I know what he means because I do that too. In fact, last week I tried to repeat the route of Kerouac's trip and do the same things he did in order to feel like him. After the convention I took some rocks home. . . . I have quite a collection of rocks now . . . " (What do you mean?)

"Well, wherever I go I bring home something, usually a rock, and I have this collection. This time I traced the outlines of the rock in my diary so that I can have it, hold on to it, know that I've been there. . . .

"You know Kerouac used to drag his mother around with him to these different places to show them to her, and in the end he went back to live with her. . . .

"When I was at the convention last week I took the occasion to drive to the next town and surprise my mother who was there . . . It's always a disappointment, like she's not really present. . . . I had a dream that I was a junior associate and she was a senior partner but she was not doing the work efficiently. I felt I would be better off doing it alone."

In fact, Peter *had* been doing the work essentially alone ever since he was a child, which is one reason why he felt so solitary even in a group. But while one can learn by oneself how to function well and one can also learn by oneself how to act like a person, one cannot learn by oneself how to *feel* like a person. To feel like a person requires the internalization of self and object representations constructed through interactions with a libidinizing maternal figure who allows both for self and mutual regulation and for partial disengagement in states of relative equilibrium.

Peter's search for an idealized lover or his creation of "Peter's world" with its secret diary were his attempts to evoke or re-create an object that would really be there to recognize him, not off in separate rooms like his parents. His efforts to remember where he had been and to feel solid as a rock by collecting rocks were concrete attempts to achieve an artificial evocative constancy that he couldn't naturally feel. Even his occasional grandiose godlike feelings were attempts to compensate for experiences of insignificance that frightened him, and he recorded them in his diary because "when I wrote down 'I am God' it didn't seem as frightening as when I was just thinking about it. . . . " Thus the diary served as an object substitute to witness, neutralize, and contain feelings that might otherwise have overwhelmed Peter.

Indeed, when the search for a substitute environmental mother does not avail, many proxies or compensatory alternatives are at hand, one of which is the secret diary. While the diary itself is by no means a pathological sign, it is often used by people with problems of constancy because, when no human is available, it can stand as a silent witness and confirmation of the reality of their thoughts and emotions, which otherwise might feel uncertain or overpowering.

For similar reasons the diary is frequently used by adolescents to help them through their phase-limited identity and constancy crises. Entries in a diary used for this purpose may mark either the highs of self-affirmation or the lows of fading self-constancy, but the sense of self is bolstered by the continuity of the ongoing entries. And this is probably why many 12-Step programs, in addition to supplying a human network, suggest that the addict keep a daily diary of his behavior and reactions in order to substitute, as it were, for the missing environmental mother who might have debriefed her toddler on the activities of the day.

Of the many famous diarists who have used their diaries at least partially for such purpose, let me cite Marlene Dietrich, an erotic icon of her time, who was given a diary by her favorite aunt at age 10½. This diary became the start of a lifelong habit of diary entries, many of which are cited in her daughter's biography (Riva 1993).

From what we know of her life (Riva 1993), Dietrich remained ever-faithful to her dutiful, constricted Prussian object-mother while simultaneously engaged in a lavish international search for the responsive environmental mother she felt lacking. As an adolescent, Dietrich recorded in this diary many fantasies of eroticized encounters with boys but also complained of her difficulty in making friends with girls. At the age of 13 she combined her first name Maria and her middle name Magdalena to invent the name Marlene for herself. This invention of herself, taken with some of the entries in her diary, suggests that a split already existed between her public and private personae.

Shortly thereafter World War I began and her father was sent to the Western Front, where he died when she was 14½. Here is her diary entry at that time:

June 1916
Now everybody is dead. Today Vati (father) will be buried.
This morning we did not go to school but to the Memorial
Cemetery to be by Vati. His grave was just being dug. It is
terribly boring here now—the only interesting boy on the
bummel (promenade) is Schmidt.

There is no further mention in the Riva biography of
her reaction to her father's death. But in December she
breaks with the aunt who had given her the diary and
who brought the news of her father's death, and simultaneously falls in love with a wounded soldier:

13 January 1917
Maybe I am a bit overexcited, but I can't help it, I love him.
With all my love . . . He is, after all, my first love. Before,
I knew nothing of love. Tomorrow, I will see you on the
promenade, Fritzi. I will see you, you, you, you angel—
you, you wonderful you . . .

But three days later she writes:

Now it's all over. The whole thing didn't mean a thing to
him . . . I'll never give myself to somebody like I did to
him, somebody who doesn't care, somebody who was
only interested to hear what a young "schoolgirl" thought
about him . . .

We may note here the progression from father to
favorite aunt to Fritzi for, although superficial and
interchangeable object relationships often occur in
early adolescence, the lack of mourning for her father is
decidedly unusual. We already see here the kind of
object inconstancy that would allow her at the height of
her fame to fall in love and be sexually involved with
several people of both sexes at the same time (Riva
1993). Ironically, she became for her cinematic public

the very elusive image that she herself was constantly seeking.

Interestingly, this type of object inconstancy was perfectly compatible with many long-term relationships and fierce and generous loyalties to people who fell into the category of narcissistic objects, as did her husband, whom she took care of throughout his life in exchange for his approval and also her daughter, Maria Riva.

After her daughter was born Dietrich gave up sex with her husband entirely, although they remained married and mutually supportive while living apart throughout most of their lives. It seems that in this she was repeating the pattern with her object mother, to whom she also remained faithful on one level while continually seeking to replace her lacking maternal functions on another. Her diary at the time was perhaps the only witness to her true feelings, even as she was becoming a Berlin celebrity:

> 18 October 1926
> The child is the only thing I have—nothing else. . . .
> Nobody understands that I am so attached to the child because nobody knows that apart from that, I have nothing. I, myself, experience nothing as a woman—nothing as a person.

This deadness of the self is an unspeakable burden from which people will flee by any means available. It is also, of course, a burden on the person who is called upon to fill the gap, as Maria Riva's biography of her mother attests. For example, Maria was called by the generic "The Child" throughout her childhood, and this nonrecognition of her as a separate and individuated person persisted in multifarious ways calculated to bolster Dietrich's public and private image of herself as a loving mother.

For the last decade or more of her life Dietrich became a pathetic recluse, living a falsely cheerful life on the telephone and sending perfumed panties to her admirers from amidst the pitiful drug-laden squalor of her hotel suite. She developed an obsessive fantasy that she was all alone and abandoned, which, by her daughter's testimony, was far from true:

> I visited her often, while her diaries stated, "I never see Maria." Each time I would note "Maria here"; each time I returned, found it crossed out with her Magic Marker. We played our little games.
>
> (Riva 1993, p. 765)

Thus Dietrich, one of the most desired women of her time, seemed at the end of her life to have regressed to her original fantasy that "I am all alone, empty and abandoned." From a psychopathological vantage point one might view her life as a brilliant hypomanic denial of this fantasy—No, I am not empty and abandoned— On the contrary, everyone in the world loves me! But the aging Dietrich, whose body was failing her, could no longer carry off the self-deception, even as she still persisted in trying to maintain the illusion in the eyes of others. Again she told the intrapsychic truth only to her diary; that just as formerly she had experienced nothing as a person and had nothing but The Child, now, since her daughter had become a separate person, even that was gone.

In this case, as in so many others, the diary acts as a repository for the true self that cannot be elsewhere revealed. When, for example, an abandoned diary is discovered years later, the writer may be astonished to recover feelings and memories that had been very successfully repressed or denied:

A man brought up in a strictly religious community had been physically and mentally abused by both parents and told that it was for his own salvation. He could remember much of the abuse but was always concerned that he might be distorting, misinterpreting, or lying to me about it. In his adolescence, searching for a witness to the truth, he had started a diary that was later forgotten. Coming upon this diary in the course of his analysis, he was struck with the acutely depressed state in which he had lived and began to feel convinced that the events he had recounted had indeed happened and were not fabrications of the Devil.

This witnessing function, whether performed by a benevolent acquaintance, a diary, or eventually the analyst, is of special importance to people whose evocative constancy is already strained and who consequently have difficulties with symbolization and with feeling an emotional certainty that something has or has not occurred. While we may not all agree with Bishop Berkeley that a tree falling unseen in the forest exists only because God is a constant witness to the events of the world, it does seem true that the conviction about an event's reality depends to some extent upon having either an external witness or some internalized confirming presence. Patients with defects in self- and object constancy do not have this confirmation and are often in doubt about the emotional or psychic reality of events, although their material reality testing *per se* may be perfectly intact.

Often this sought-for confirmation may present as a functional attribute like the image of someone's face or eyes or, as in the following examples, as the sound of an idealized voice or the odor of the beloved.

In the last few decades a product of modern technology, the telephone answering machine, has proven of value in the management of many patients with difficulties of evocative constancy. Frequently in the early course of treatment, these patients may call at any time of day or night with an insignificant message or without leaving any message at all, simply to hear the analyst's voice. Although by now when this occurs I can usually tell who has called and about how long the phase might last, I have not found it of value to confront this practice. In the normal course of analysis it is usually self-containing and the facts will eventually emerge, often accompanied by material recounting how early tentative attempts to use some person as a confirmation of self-constancy were rebuffed.

Indeed the concrete use of a diary or telephone message to hold on to fading self- or object constancy is paralleled in our culture by the frequent concrete use of video and television to replace a diminished capacity for fantasy.

A gay professional man had throughout his life needed to use sadomasochistic videos in order to masturbate. In the course of analysis one could watch the growth of his evocative constancy as he first began to value his analyst and then miss her and then think about what she might be doing. This evolution of object constancy was paralleled by a firming up of self-constancy and a development of fantasy life so that ongoing fantasies and feelings of sexual desire came to replace his concrete need for S-M videos.

It is worth emphasizing that the growth of evocative constancy in the course of analysis leads not only to an increase of self-constancy but also to the development of higher symbolic processes and a greater ability to use fantasy as a carrier of desire and not only of projections. For example, the patient mentioned here had used frequent masturbation to porno videos as a way of propping up his failing sense of self, partly because an intense orgasm is one of the easiest ways to reaffirm the sense of "I am." As his sense of his and the analyst's ongoing existence became more firm, he was able to entertain fantasies of desire for her and by extension, for others. But one can note a similar evolution in cases of less severe pathology as well:

> Arthur was brought up in a country inn where his parents worked. Every few days the guests changed and a new set arrived; his parents were constantly preoccupied with caring for the guests and utilized Arthur for this purpose. Distracted and narcissistic, they were neither constant nor reliable objects. In Arthur's world the one thing that remained the same was the natural environment, the terrain, and he memorized the form and location of every strawberry patch, every honeysuckle bush, every rock, and every tree. He knew them intimately and would return to them incessantly for comfort, for they represented his background of safety and one of the few constancies in his life. The day that I left on a short vacation he dreamed that these rocks behind the inn were crumbling. He once said: "My parents are like a hard, slick, smooth surface—you can make no imprint on them and you can't tell who you are or verify what's happening by the impression you leave. But analysis is like a patch of moss; it's soft and you can press yourself into it and you feel who you are by the way it enfolds you."

It turned out that as a child when Arthur felt particularly deadened by the unresponsiveness of his parents, he used to go outside and sit for a long time watching the patch of moss that grew behind the inn.

Frequently one sees patients who gaze longingly at one's face before lying down or on leaving the hour, as if to imprint its impression on their memory. Others may suffer from prosopagnosia, a difficulty in remembering faces. Almost always these are people who have had some problem with evocative constancy. Often enough they were children whose mothers were either depressed or subject to unpredictable rages, and their prolonged gazing may be an attempt either to merge with the depressed mother, to pull her back into the world, or to search for signs of her impending rage. One patient said to me:

> I watch your face all the time . . . sometimes it's happy and smiling, sometimes it's caring and concerned, and sometimes you look tired and exhausted. I look at faces and I have a feeling of loss and I can't let go because it won't be there anymore . . . the same face won't be there again because people change . . .

This woman's mother had been unpredictably depressed and angry when the child was very young and even in second grade, when mother was away, the little girl would get frightened and go to Mommy's room and steal her pillow, scented with perfume, to sleep on. The smell of Mommy's perfume was always comfortingly the same and she could use this constant attribute of Mommy's body to calm herself and sleep.

Another patient, when asked about a suspicious glance he cast at me, explained:

> I have to tell you, I'm always afraid that people will turn weird on me. I keep worrying that they'll leave the room and when they come back things will have changed completely . . . I suppose it's because I would leave my "happy" home and when I came back my brothers were crying, my father was crazy and my mother was looking desperately at me to do something . . .

Actually, what this patient was remembering was the screen that covered much earlier episodes of inconstancy in the second and third years of life. He had never had an actual object loss in his childhood, but rather many repeated experiences of object failure with consequent experiences of loss of continuity of the self in both space and time.

Patients like this complain of feeling "spacey," and they may also complain of losing things, especially watches or other items that connect them to "reality," and of not being able to keep track of time or of vital information. Others may have developed an early precocious reaction formation and become obsessed with defining their position in time and space and regulating their mental functioning with an absolute precision.

Those patients who are chronically anxious that people or things might turn "weird" on them become very attached to happy moments out of fear that they are soon doomed to disappear. A patient complained bitterly that after intercourse with her new boyfriend, instead of lying there and savoring the moment, he answered the telephone and became engaged in a lively conversation with the caller. After exploring the usual differences in this respect between men and women, it eventually became clear that her desperate need to preserve such moments of pleasure and happiness related to her profound belief that these moments might never come again, whereas her boyfriend seemed confident that their happy experience would be repeated tomorrow. These patients recall Faust's cry: *Verweile doch, du bist so schön,* for they cling to the moment out of fear that it may never come again.

Interestingly, those patients whose early environment has somehow failed to provide them with an adequate sense of their own continuity in time and space are often oblivious to the extent to which their environment deviated from the norm. I recall one patient whose mother, when she should have been sending her off to school in the morning, was instead in bed, inebriated, depressed, and unwakeable. Finally one day this little girl desperately asked her classmates: "How do the rest of you manage to wake your mothers up in the morning?" Another patient, whose mother constantly rearranged his bedroom while the little boy was away at school, thought that sleeping in a different position every few weeks was the normal thing to do. Both these patients had what in fairness could only be called loving and devoted object mothers, but mothers whose own narcissism and inability to self-regulate disabled them from providing an optimal growth environment.

Up to now I have spoken chiefly about the mothering functions as observed through the narcissistic disorders, but of course fathers exist not only to support functions such as primary maternal preoccupation but importantly in their own right from early on (Abelin 1975, Klein 1948). Historically, fathering functions have been conceived of as reality oriented: the call to wake rather than to sleep (Lewin 1950), to work rather than to play, to function rather than to just be (Winnicott 1971), to conquer rather than to affiliate (Tannen 1990) and to be sexual rather than sensual. How much of this traditional division of function will survive social change is difficult to say, although certain functions appear to be biologically linked to some extent.

But far more important than role attribution is the structural significance of arriving at the triadic position. For object constancy can never be fully achieved within the exclusive dyadic framework even by an idyllic relationship to a resonating or attuned object. The dyad can exist in relative isolation, but the triad brings us fully into the world of struggle, conflict, and reality, the world that in conventional notation has been called the father's world.

For attunement carried beyond its time leaves no space to grow and the good-enough mother, by requiring the child to provide signals and cues as its capabilities grow, is introducing reality into the dyad. Thus, by leaving a space for reality to enter, the mother is creating a "paternal" interval, father "principle," or third force that takes on the persecutory aspect of the father even though an actual father may be absent. This third force is persecutory not only because, like the serpent, it disturbs the dyadic Eden but also because, as the unseen other, it becomes the projected carrier of unacceptable, disavowed, and murderous impulses.

While on one hand this paternal force protects against engulfment in the maternal matrix, on the other hand it is only in struggling with the persecutory father that full object constancy and symbolization is achieved. We have all seen innumerable examples of people who are momentarily refueled in therapeutic or life situations but where the emotional refueling doesn't last. Often the failure of dyadic refueling may relate to the suppression, disavowal, or denigration of the persecutory paternal figure (Chasseguet-Smirgel 1983), and it is only after the reintegration of this figure that a more durable symbolization and constancy can be achieved. It is the struggle to achieve this dynamic triadic balance and the search for and flight from the paternal function that often gives rise to the monsters and golems discussed in Chapter 6.

But here I am concerned primarily with the earlier and more primitive search for the maternal functions. I have tried to differentiate two levels on which this occurs: the level of the narcissistic and perverse patient who is libidinized and possesses a symbolic object or self-object and the level of the severe addict, bulorectic, or psychosomatic patient where libidinization and symbolization may be profoundly arrested. These patients, for whom psychic deadness is a way of life, live in a state of inner emptiness or desymbolization (Freedman and Berzofsky 1994). They lack a sense of their existence in the world and a sense of the real existence of others. Their lives feel like bloodless charades; they experience themselves as from another planet, moving like wraiths amongst people who seem not to notice that they belong to a different species. Patients on the extreme of this continuum are nonlibidinized, never having experienced the touch that awakens the infant's sensual being to a love of its own body and a certainty of its existence. They have never arrived at a consistent feeling of I AM (Winnicott 1965), and they move through the world like vampires, constantly seeking in fantasy or actuality to validate their existence through the blood and flesh of others, as if attempting by vampirism to regain the libido they never had.

An extraordinary literary example may be found in the novel *Perfume* by Patrick Suskind (1986). This is the story of the monster Grenouille who was cast aside for dead by his mother and never nurtured. Never possessing the odor of a human being, he devotes his career to recapturing this libidinal essence, first by becoming a master perfumer and then by murdering beautiful women to steal the odor that makes them beloved.

Unfortunates of this kind do exist, and not only in the literary imagination, but they rarely come to the analyst's attention. They are extreme examples of a normal process gone awry, of a delibidinization and desymbolization so horrifying as to be almost unimaginable.

I have suggested in Chapter 3 that perversion is a behavioral manifestation of the compression of psychic space and that one pathway to object love leads to the creation and enlargement of psychic and transitional space. Another way of putting this is that perversion, entropy, or Thanatos is the shrinking of psychic space and the consequent loss of symbolization, whereas Eros is the creation and enlargement of psychic space and symbolization, since the libidinal object becomes our first symbol.

I have mentioned how in the well-synchronized mother–infant couple an open space emerges in which disengagement from the system becomes possible and in which the infant begins to consolidate his own agency. Thus a life of one's own begins in a space of one's own, made safe from internal and external impingements and libidinized by the care the mother has lavished on the infant's psyche-soma.

But for those who have never known good-enough care and the sense of I AM it engenders, the choices are difficult. They can turn to extreme forms of sadism or delinquency (Winnicott 1984) to capture a sense of aliveness or hold fast to the fading images of object or self, or they can sink into an automatized existence that may look real but feels unbearably empty and dead. If they come to us for help we attempt, in essence, both to libidinize them and to provide an adequate environment for growth.

Libidinization occurs naturally as the transference develops, although the resistance and the unalloyed aggression in these cases is likely to be extreme. The provision of an adequate environment occurs through the analytic framework, through optimal enactment and play and through encouraging the continuities and discontinuities of normal development to establish a dynamic mutual equilibrium and create a libidinized potential space. The difficulties of this work are enormous, made doubly so by the chaotic conditions under which these people often live.

But practical difficulties aside, we seem to have come some distance in our understanding since Freud first noted those desymbolizing patients who would "tolerate no surrogates" and respond only to the "logic of soup with dumplings for arguments." (1915, p. 167). What he then attributed to "an elemental passionateness" we might now see as part of a concrete narcissistic or perverse thought disorder whose developmental origins we are just beginning to understand. And although our therapy is still both arduous and time-consuming, the interaction of therapy and research offers us hope for the treatment of those disorders of evocative constancy that lead to an endless search for the parental functions hidden under the guise of an elusive image.

CHAPTER 5

Rhythmicities, Transitions, and States of Consciousness

PEOPLE HAVE STYLES OF waking up just as they have styles of departure; some are wide awake at the first sound of the alarm or say goodbye with a firm clasp and turn on their heels and leave. Others linger at their host's door or at the gates of sleep and cycle slowly through the stages of departure or awakening. Whether we awaken abruptly or in stages, as we make the transition from sleep to waking state we check ourselves out much as a computer checks its memory and system on booting up, making sure that the parts of our body are present and functional and that we are oriented as to place, time, and person. This is perhaps the commonest example of a transition from one state of consciousness to another, followed by reorienting or "grounding" behavior.

Waking and sleeping states, lethargic or hyperactive states, drugged or intoxicated states, states of boredom, creativity, and sexual excitement are all ordinary examples of alterations from the normal state of consciousness. But I believe that the normal state of consciousness is a popular fiction and that most people are normally cycling back and forth through a multitude of states, with greater or lesser success.

We may define a state of consciousness or behavioral state as a pattern of physiological and psychological parameters that occur together, repeat themselves, and are relatively stable and enduring over time (Putnam 1989, 1992, Rapaport 1951a,b). Because there is no generally accepted way of describing or classifying states of consciousness, I will begin by listing and illustrating what seem to me some of the more important parameters, based on Rapaport (ibid.). These include:

A. *A particular pattern of arousal and affect*

Here the classic example is manic-depressive disorder, which can show a startling shift from hyperarousal and manic affect to lethargy and depressed affect. But patients with multiple personality disorders frequently have alter egos that are known by their affect—the angry one, the caring one—or by their arousal level— the tired one, the overexcited one, and so forth. And all of us have either voluntarily or involuntarily experienced states of special lethargy or alertness with accompanying changes of mood.

B. *A particular body schema and orientation in space and time*

As we fall asleep we can feel our body schema "melting," and this body schema feels different from the sense of our body when we are energetically walking, or when our body is prosthetically extended, as on stilts or in driving a car. Likewise our orientation in space and time is markedly different when fighting gravity or succumbing to it, when making love or when engaged in a tax audit.

C. *A particular organization of thought and language, including a particular organization of memory and amnesias*

Free association on the couch alters our language and thought organization in ways that have been extensively studied by psychoanalysis. Drug intoxication, hypnogogic and hypnopompic states, traumatic states, REM states, and other states alter both thought and language; it is commonly more difficult to communicate rationally with someone who is drunk, sleepy, or traumatized.

Memory and amnesias are altered in fugue states, in *déjà vu* and *déjà raconté,* in reconstruction and recovery of childhood amnesias, and so on. In multiple personality disorder the alternate personalities differ in the time periods for which they have memory, in the "facts" that are remembered, and in the access they have to the memories of other personalities.

D. *A particular type of reflective awareness or a particular dialectic between subjective and objective self-awareness*

Here we can be either totally lost in our own subjective awareness and oblivious to others and to our location in time and space, or we can be acutely aware of observing ourselves as if we were another person, sometimes to the extent of losing the sense of our own reality. Normally we are engaged in a dialectic between these two poles, a dialectic dependent upon and appropriate to circumstances.

E. *A particular degree of agency,*
   intentionality, or spontaneity

This refers to the extent to which our experiences feel more passive, such as "it's happening to me," or more active, such as "I'm doing it." Here again we normally alternate between different degrees of agency, but the extremes of this continuum may be seen in pathologies such as infantile personality or hyper grandiosity.

F. *Particular thresholds of sensitivity and a*
   specific aesthetic of attention that prefers
   certain sensory modalities and forms of
   organization

This aesthetic reflects both genetic gifts, levels of fixation, and the language of interaction in the early maternal matrix. Certain patients are extraordinarily sensitive to smell and can identify not only the previous occupant of the couch but also their mood without having seen them—"This person must be depressed if he smells that way." Other people are almost oblivious to certain modalities of perception, while the loss of one modality, as in deafness or blindness, may lead to astonishing sensitivities in other areas.

G. *A particular pattern of transition from*
   one state to another and a pattern of
   reorienting behavior or "grounding" that
   accompanies or follows each transition

Although we now have considerable data from the observation of multiple personality disorders (Putnam

1992), the previous century offered equivalent data from religious and trance states (James [1896] 1984), and Eastern meditative literature has been extensively concerned with this subject for centuries.

H. *A particular sense of self, which may be conceptualized as the pattern of relationships among all of the above parameters*

I am hypothesizing that when all of these parameters can be specified, we will have defined a sense of self that may be experienced as relatively constant or as radically changeable, depending upon the genetics, intensities, and the dialectic between the parameters.

Even in the beginning we are able to distinguish variations in the infant's behavioral states, such as alert inactivity, waking activity, crying, regular sleep and paradoxical sleep (Wolff 1987). The basic polarity between sleep and waking is given from birth, but an intricate system of infant–parent coordination ensues in which the caretaker reacts to the infant's change of state in an effort to nurture, modulate, and establish a relative equilibrium. From the beginning this system is interactive, the caretaker affecting the infant's states and the infant affecting the caretaker's states, as anyone who has spent sleepless nights with a neonate will remember. The ongoing regulation of the system seems based on an integration of self and mutual regulation (Beebe and Lachman 1988). In the first few weeks of life the normal infant is in a state of absolute dependence, and the mother is in a complementary state of "primary maternal preoccupation" (Winnicott 1965). While the infant is capable of discriminating and learning even from the beginning, a good deal of his time is spent in vegetative functions such as eating and sleeping and in developing a psychobiological life and self-organization (Ellman 1992, Jacobson 1964).

If good-enough synchrony is achieved there emerges by three weeks an adapted system with an "open space" (Sander 1983). This means that the infant is "regulated," fed, dry, and comfortable but not yet ready to return to sleep and the mother is visible but otherwise occupied: the infant is not "taken over" by either internal or external stimuli. In this time of alert inactivity in which the system is in relative equilibrium but there is momentary disengagement from interaction, an open or potential space emerges in which the infant can learn to consolidate his own agency and to begin his creative life (Jacobson 1964, Sander 1983, Winnicott 1965).

What the mother has done by being attuned to the infant is to promote the tendency of the inborn psychic apparatus to create structures. She has generated a space insulating the infant from both external and internal stimulation, " . . . without the infant's options to *select* and intiate action being preempted by the demands of *basic regulation*." Sander feels that " . . . self has a particular relation to the initiation of behavior and to the negotiation of agency in relation to states of relative equilibrium in the individual's care-giving system" (Sander 1983, pp. 344–345).

Thus the infant's awareness of himself develops gradually out of the regulated mother–infant matrix. His need for the breast is met neither too late nor too soon, but at precisely the time that will allow him to experience and identify drives and objects at an optimal level, neither too weak to be noticed nor so strong as to disorganize (Loewald 1960, 1971, Stern 1985, Winnicott 1965).

The infant begins his life largely in sleep and must learn to organize and differentiate his waking and his sleeping states. In the process he begins to organize and contain REM phenomena so that increasing periods of alert wakefulness become available for mutual gazing, vocalizing, and smiling (Ellman 1992). The extensively differentiated waking states of the normal adult are all developmental and maturational achievements. They are self-organizing and self-equilibrating states, which may be reversed or surrendered in a voluntary or involuntary regression. Indeed, some adults may never have achieved a full range of differentiated states (Bach 1977). In the ontogenesis of these states, the task of the parent seems threefold:

1. To facilitate the development of a variety of differentiated waking and sleeping states,
2. To encourage self-regulation of these states so that they are stable and context appropriate, and
3. To encourage the integration of these states so that the transitions between them are relatively smooth and the sense of self remains relatively stable throughout.

Our normal states of consciousness may be thought of as the heritage of our mutual interactions with the early environmental mother, for they "hold" us in our daily life in a way sometimes analogous to the way we were held both physically and mentally by our first caregivers. Of course, these interactions are mutually reorganized at each developmental stage and reacquired, transformed, and reintegrated at higher developmental levels.

In the course of a depth analysis the analyst may often be tempted to "read" this backwards and derive insights about the early mother-of-environment from fluctuations and conflicts around states of consciousness. But concrete correlations between early environment and adult pathology can be both enormously illuminating and also dangerous, since they may neglect the interactional restructuring that transforms the participants over time.

Although our normal waking states of consciousness are derived from the early maternal environmental matrix, they are significantly modified in the course of development, and they also require both internal and external input or "nutriments" to maintain themselves. I have noted that with a good-enough psychobiological beginning the mother–infant system reaches a state of equilibrium that allows for transitory disengagements from interaction and the creation of a free interval. This open space enables the infant to develop a self-organization by developing a sense of distance between his self and his objects and between his self and his own needs or instincts. Normal development produces both internal and external continuities and discontinuities: internal disturbances such as pangs of hunger and external disturbances such as separation and loss. There are mothers who create pathology because they don't attend sufficiently to these disruptions and others who create pathology because they don't allow these disruptions to occur. The good-enough mother makes her higher level of organization available to the child, who then uses this to develop his own organization and awareness of his objects and needs.

Psychic organizers such as disengagement and the creation of space are dependent on the continuities and discontinuities of sleep rhythms, circadian rhythms, hormonal rhythms, satiation rhythms, and other rhythms, and on the optimal regulation of such rhythmic oscillations. It is not only attachments that matter, but attachments, disengagements, and reattachments; the optimal interruption and resumption of naturally occurring rhythmicities. It is this that builds structures, and to the extent that this is disrupted, one sees a dedifferentiation and a failure of organizers and subsequent regulation. In analysis with the more disturbed patients we attempt through play, through enactment, and through the analytic frame to regenerate and reestablish these normally occurring rhythmicities, these continuities and discontinuities that we hope will create the kind of space that might have occurred in optimal development.

The traumatized infant who is bombarded by stimuli and overwhelmed with anxiety is unable to respond spontaneously and has lost all sense of agency. At best he can learn to respond mechanically to the world. At the beginning of an analysis with a very traumatized adult, he may often try to eliminate all naturally occurring rhythmicities and to "freeze" the analytic situation into a rigid mode that will guarantee against further discontinuity and trauma. I have described such a patient in Chapter 3: the young man who would not allow me to say a word for many months. At the beginning of the analysis we may choose to accept this condition and allow the patient his delusionally omnipotent control of the transference, in the hope that if we accept in the right way long enough he may eventually feel empowered enough to allow for a thrust of development and to take a risk with discontinuity.

These patients have been traumatically overstimulated and are seeking quiet; others have been traumatically understimulated and are seeking to be aroused from a marasmus-like condition and to have some feeling of aliveness and love placed within their body parts. These patients as infants may have been deprived of maternal attention and may have stimulated themselves through rocking, self scratching, hair pulling and other compensatory behaviors (Novick and Novick 1987). If the interaction continues in this way, it may in later years lead to a developing self-destructive line of anorexia, bulimia, delicate self cutting, and other attempts at self-stimulation and self-regulation.

Adults who are stimulus deprived in Arctic camp, in prison, or in sensory deprivation experiments seem to avidly crave *any* external stimulation: Bexton's (1954) isolation subjects were eager to listen to ordinarily boring stock reports. Others tend to regress and to compensate by generating internal stimulation such as somatizations or hallucinations. This stimulus hunger makes sensory-deprived people highly susceptible to indoctrination and brainwashing. But it is also a good example of the observation that different states of consciousness process information in nonlinear, radically different ways, so that a stock report that may be boring in one state can seem highly exciting in another, or a pacifier or caress that seems soothing or welcome in one state may feel intrusive in another (Putnam 1992, Rapaport 1951a, Wolff 1987). It seems clear that there are individual limits of tolerance for stimulus overload and deprivation, that there is an optimal range for both internal and external stimulation, and that infants on extremes of the continuum may require extraordinary parenting to survive well (Ellman 1992, Suomi 1991). It is within the range that is optimal for both infant and caretaker that attuned mutual regulation is achieved.

In this respect the infant observers or ''babywatchers'' have given us many fascinating paradigms, especially that of mutual gazing, which illustrates so dramatically the processes of both self and mutual regulation (Brazelton et al. 1974). Of special interest is the paradigm of the caretaker who will not permit gaze avoidance or disengagement, leading to "chase and dodge" (Beebe and Stern 1977), a condition in which the mother continually pursues the infant who continually seeks to avoid her. Here the mutual regulation structure may be intact, but the pair may still be misattuned and the infant may be constantly struggling to achieve self-regulation (Beebe and Lachmann 1988). Such situations ultimately lead to confusion and despair. Worse yet, they deprive the child of the opportunity to momentarily disengage from interaction in the system while self-regulated and thus to create for himself a free or open space.

In most cases the resultant attempts at compensation will be characterized by erratic shifts and oscillations because the child or patient will not have learned to smoothly reconcile endogenous and exogenous stimulation into a well-integrated set of states of consciousness. For just as in the ideal psyche the distinctions between id, ego, and superego are least visible, so in the ideal psyche the transition between states of consciousness is seamless and we must look to pathology, to instances of flawed or erratic switching to reveal the mechanisms involved.

It was thus no accident that a patient whom one might now diagnose with a multiple personality disorder, Anna O., was the one who first opened the door to our view of altered states of consciousness, of psychoanalytic technique, and of the unconscious. We remember that Anna O. spoke only German in one state of consciousness but understood only English in another and had to be induced into a specific hypnotic state before she could recall certain traumatic memories. Of course, there is now an accumulation of experimental evidence suggesting that events are more easily recalled in the specific state of consciousness in which they were first learned or experienced rather than in other states, for example Bower (1981). We may also recall the Chaplin film in which Charlie befriends a millionaire who offers him hospitality and fortune when they are both drunk, but who doesn't recognize him and has him ejected when sober, only to become his best friend again when drunk. State-specific learning and memory has implications for analytic technique that I shall touch on later.

Multiple personality disorder, which is a natural laboratory for studying states of consciousness, fell out of favor in psychoanalysis for reasons that were apparently both theoretical and political. Freud's early decision to emphasize repression over vertical splitting, as well as his decision to emphasize seduction fantasies over the incidence of actual seduction led to a lessening of interest in both multiple personalities and altered states (Ellenberger 1970, Putnam 1989). Now that our consciousness has been expanded so that we can easily encompass both horizontal and vertical splitting (Freud 1940, Kohut 1971), as well as both actual and fantasied seduction, we are in a better position to understand alter personalities and states of consciousness.

Investigators who have studied multiple personality disorder have been impressed with two phenomena that can sometimes be observed with the change from one personality to another: *switching* behavior and *grounding* behavior. A personality switch in MPD may be signaled by a blink or upward roll of the eyes, a twitch or grimace of the face, or a bodily shudder, posture change, or even convulsion. Switching behavior may often be disguised, concealed, or integrated into other movements (Putnam 1989, 1992).

Once a new personality or state of consciousness has emerged, the patient may touch his face or chair, press his temples, scan the room or shift posture restlessly. This has been conceptualized as a kind of "grounding" or reorientation process for the new personality (Putnam ibid.).

A recent series of studies by Freedman and Berzofsky (1994) is of interest in this respect. They videotaped sessions of dynamic psychotherapy with the camera focused on the therapists. They observed that significant interventions, transference interpretations, or dynamic formulations by the therapists were preceded by a particular kinesic response sequence. Such an action sequence was comprised of a foot kick, postural rearrangement, or self-touching. In a summary statement, Freedman concluded: "It appears that the therapist, through this rhythmically-organized action sequence needed to recreate that kind of inner space which allowed her to formulate, select and implement the intervention."

I would suggest that the switching and grounding behavior associated with personality switches in MPD and the muted but similar behavior in therapists before an intervention are both associated with a shift in states of consciousness. I have reported similar reorientation behavior in narcissistic patients at moments of transition as, for example, when entering or leaving the analytic session (Bach 1977). It now seems understandable that a shift in state of consciousness that involves a change in awareness, in sense of agency, in language and thought, in thresholds, and in body schema should require a brief or even extensive period of reorientation. And it is precisely in cases such as multiple personality or manic-depressive disorder, where the integration of different states of consciousness is most problematic, that we see the most extensive switching and grounding behavior. And just as the patient attempts to "ground" or reorient *himself* after each switch, so analytic trust may need to be reestablished in the treatment dyad after each switch of state, of personality, or of transference paradigm.

There is some reason to believe that transitional switching and grounding behavior would be more often observed if we were alert to the possibility of its occurrence, as were Freedman and his colleagues when they focused their videocamera on the therapist. Clearly, observation of patient–therapist couples comparable to our observation of mother–infant couples would have much to teach us about the reciprocal dynamics of therapeutic interaction. Freedman apparently suggests that the therapist, before making an interpretation, needs to create a kind of inner space relatively free from both internal and external press. If so, this might be a later transformation of the free space the infant first achieves when he momentarily disengages from the equilibrated mother–infant system (Sander 1983), the precursor of the spontaneous gesture and the creative act. This, of course, touches on the as yet fairly mysterious issue of the emergence of new behavioral functions and forms in the course of ontogenesis. It may be worth noting that phase transitions, emergent and transcendant phenomena, self-organizing systems, and dynamic regulation between order and chaos are concepts that play an important role in the study of complexity (Waldrop 1992), a field that deals with emergent patterns common to all the sciences.

Leaving speculation aside, we may nonetheless note the value of attending to reciprocal changes of states of consciousness in the patient–analyst system during the course of analysis. We might, for example, understand

Freud's (1912) "free-floating attention" or Isakower's (1963) "analyzing instrument" as injunctions to the analyst to join the patient in his particular state of consciousness so that their language and thought organizations as well as memory retrieval systems will be operating on similar rather than disparate structural levels. This matching of states of consciousness may be the best guarantee that both patient and analyst will understand each other and that the analyst will not be speaking German to someone who can understand only English.

It would then seem likely that certain technical analytic procedures such as holding are best done in a state of consciousness similar to the patient's, whereas others, such as transference interpretations, are best done in a different state of consciousness. In holding, for example, the analyst might ideally strive to attain a state of consciousness in which language, thought organization, and thresholds are similar to the patient's, in which self-awareness is largely subjective, a sense of agency minimal, and in which body schema is supportive and conforming. This would be part of a larger psychobiological attunement with the patient and, indeed, a number of women analysts have told me that during holding the patient's menstrual cycle has become synchronized with their own, or vice versa.

Likewise, an empathic response might require similar parameters so that the analyst would be attuned to the patient, but self-awareness would oscillate between subjective and objective to enable the analyst to scrutinize her own identifications with the patient.

When making transference interpretations, by contrast, the analyst would ideally assume a state in which language and thought organization are at the next higher level of abstraction from the patient's, in which self-awareness is largely objective, agency maximized, and body schema differentiated. A shift to the empathic state might then be required in order to gauge the effects of the intervention or to reestablish trust, with a return to the interpretive state if one were trying to show, for example, that the structure of the response confirms the interpretation.

One could easily envisage a cartography or taxonomy of states of consciousness in both patient and analyst, with particular attention to the interaction between the patient's state and the analyst's. For example, some time ago Kohut (1971) noted that patients in an altered "narcissistic" state of consciousness were frequently able to induce an altered state of boredom in their analyst. This is now a clinical commonplace, with emphasis on the patient's suppressed anger or the anger he induces in us; on his re-creation of a childhood situation in which he was not responded to, or on his emotional withdrawal and exclusion of us from his subjective world, thereby arousing our antipathy to being used as a self-object. I believe these dynamic formulations are all accurate and extremely useful, but it might also be clinically helpful to understand the structure inducing this phenomenon.

We have seen in Chapter 2 that the overinflated type narcissistic patient is predominantly in a state of subjective awareness, totally and enthusiastically immersed in what he is doing, and that the deflated narcissistic type is predominantly in a state of objective self-awareness, critically observing and reflecting upon himself. In either case we experience him as peculiarly absorbed in himself because he doesn't oscillate between subjective and objective awareness as most people do. Even when he does pay attention to us, it is usually to enlist our enthusiastic mirroring of his subjective excitement or our judgmental agreement with his objective self-criticism. In either case he is relating to us as a functional self-object to support his fixated state of consciousness. For to relate to us as a person rather than as a function he would have to relate to himself in a multidimensional way, oscillating between multiple perspectives on himself and on us.

Thus the dynamic reasons for our boredom have structural correlates. We are bored with the narcissist because he is not freely cycling back and forth between states of consciousness, thereby depriving us of the ordinary shifts in perspective that, though mostly unnoticed, provide an important part of our sense of aliveness and three-dimensionality in life. For much as our perpetual eye movements serve to keep the retina "refreshed," whereas immobilization leads to disturbances of vision, so we imagine the continual cycling of states of consciousness to be necessary for the maintenance of normal mental functioning.

As in so many areas of functioning, a dynamic balance seems to be a critical factor. On the one hand we have multiple personalities with seemingly erratic shifts between states and between different selves, and on the other hand we have certain obsessive or narcissistic patients so rigidly fixated to one state of consciousness that they seem like automatons or mechanical men (Bach 1975). Clearly, our current vision of normality requires some dynamic balance between order and chaos, between the ability to freely cycle between alternate states and the necessity of maintaining some integration among these states.

I have mentioned that one of the tasks of parenting is to encourage the development of a variety of states of consciousness, to help regulate these states so that they are stable and appropriate, and to promote the integration of these states so that the transitions are smooth and the sense of self remains constant throughout. Here is a case where these tasks were not well performed and some of the issues that arose:

> When Anne first came to see me she noted that she was a slow awakener and remained in a hypnopompic state for some time after the alarm rang. Sometimes when she was making the morning coffee she would have a sudden "flash" of being hit on the head, or as she was riding the train she might "image" the car exploding. Slowly we learned that these were not typical obsessional thoughts but rather state-specific remnants of a traumatic assault on her mind that she suffered as a child. At other times she would go into a frenetic state in which she became totally focused on accomplishing some task to the exclusion of everything else in the world. We learned that these states occurred when she felt guiltily obliged to "save" a situation, as she had felt obliged to rescue herself and her brother from their mother's potential explosions.
>
> Anne grew up with a manic-depressive mother and a father who was well intentioned but absent, disorganized, and sadly neglectful. The family lived on the cusp of disorganization with the radio constantly blaring and people shouting; Anne was frequently late to school, and when school was out she was supposed to be picked up but was often forgotten. Even as an adult the terror and humiliation of these times can still bring tears to her eyes.
>
> Anne has, by dint of unusual intelligence, character, and enormous personal effort, managed to become a highly regarded partner in a prominent firm, responsible for ongoing multimillion-dollar decisions. Unless one knew her intimately it would be impossible to guess at the level of anxiety that sometimes lies beneath the surface. She still carries this early environmental turmoil around in her waking consciousness, not as a "background of safety" (Sandler 1960), but as a continual background of disorganization.
>
> Anne is still engaged in learning how to self-regulate and to mutually regulate in a system with her boyfriend. But

even as a child in the chaos of her home, she would try to find a hiding place in the attic or behind the couch where she could calm herself and gather her thoughts together. In this open space, disengaged from the manic-depressive system, she could begin to feel that her emotions and her sense of self and objects were her own and not simply reactions to external impingements. Later on she was able to find a safe place at boarding school with a group of girls to whom she remains fiercely loyal to this day. Still later she worked abroad at her firm's European office, and that country became for her what her home had never been, a repository of safe feelings and loving nostalgia. Cases like this impress one with the powerful need to find a space in which the self can grow, an urge that may start in the mother–infant game of "chase and dodge" but that can, through innumerable transformations, eventually work itself out on an international playing field.

Indeed, the frequent examples we see of patients who lead secret lives or search for a secret place of their own may often enough refer to a childhood where privacy was continually violated and the child engaged in a constant fight to maintain his equilibrium, never knowing the luxury of a space in which to create his own world. One of my patients kept a secret diary whose existence was revealed only well into the analysis. Analytically, the blank page could be traced back to the search for a quiet space, hidden from the family turmoil. One of the accomplishments of treatment was the ultimate integration of this private self with the rest of his life.

Unintegrated persona or states of consciousness are almost always experienced as shameful or "crazy" and consequently may remain hidden for a long time. But many patients from backgrounds that encouraged splitting rather than state unification have created secret worlds that they either live in or visit from time to time.

These worlds may be populated by androids, human-oids, ghosts, imaginary companions, Tolkeinian charac-ters, or equivalents (Bach 1985, Chapter 6), but they belong to the deepest self that for various reasons has been unable to see the light of day. The stabilization and integration of these states remains a primary task for the psychoanalyst, not only in obvious cases of multiple personality but also in their far more frequent presen-tation in the less severe character disorders. Often attentional problems and learning difficulties are symp-toms of narcissistic character disorder and may clear in analysis without any direct confrontation. But even patients with true learning disabilities and attention deficit disorders may find it helpful to understand their states of consciousness and their difficulties in being quietly alert. Frequently the learning disablity has made these patients ashamed of their internal states and of elements of their inner self, and they can often be helped, sometimes dramatically, to overcome this.

Many patients have been related to as narcissistic extensions or as functions by their caretakers, which is another way of saying that they have not been allowed a safe, disengaged space of their own in which to develop. When we see such patients they may appear to have instinctual conflicts, which they may, but some do not even "own" the instincts with which to have such conflicts. They may also act as if they have real selves, sometimes worldly successful ones, but for some these selves feel like decoys concealing the hiding place in which their last hope for a real life lies hidden. These patients have little trust and a tremendous fear of dependency. They do not feel valuable unless they are useful and functional objects for their analyst as they were for their parents, and they expect to be discarded like Kleenex when their function has been served. The integration of their split-off states of consciousness, alternate selves, and fragmentary personae is intimately connected with accepting them as genuine whole people and not as subjects in a therapeutic experiment of whatever persuasion. These people have already had enough of being objects in someone else's life. They need a life of their own.

A life of one's own begins in a space of one's own, made safe from external and internal impingements. This safety is first guaranteed by a good-enough caretaker and later, perhaps, by a good-enough analyst. In this space one is free to adventure, explore, and experiment, among other things, with altered states of consciousness.

It has long been known and amply documented that altered states may be used for defensive purposes (Dickes 1965, Ferenczi 1988, Fliess 1953, Stein 1965), and one of the earliest controversies in psychoanalysis concerned the defensive use of the "hypnoid" state (Breuer and Freud 1893–1895). I have elsewhere (Bach 1985) extensively discussed narcissistic states as both fixations and defensive regressions, and it is common enough to see patients from sexually abused or traumatized backgrounds who use altered states to defend against the trauma. It has even become street knowledge that drug or alcohol intoxication may be used to self-medicate for depression. What has been less amply discussed, at least in the psychoanalytic literature, is the use of altered states for purposes of tension release and self-exploration. In defensive or compensatory use, one starts from a feeling of unpleasure and is searching for a state of well-being, whereas in exploratory or transcendent usage, one starts from a feeling of well-being and is searching for a change of state that will open unknown doors.

We know, for example, that children who haven't received enough skin contact to adequately demarcate their boundaries and foster individuation may sometimes engage in spinning or twirling as a support for their sense of separateness. But we also see normal children who search for "highs" through bodily motion: they "play" at turning in circles until dizzy or work themselves into a state of exhilaration by swinging, jumping, tickling, and group excitement. Even infants at play seem to generate moments of intense excitement, "highs" that they eventually learn to modulate because they can become frightening. They stop being frightening as the child learns to regulate them or as they become regulated in the parental or therapeutic dyad. But right from the beginning there appears to be a tendency to seek or to play with experiences of altered states.

Indeed, it seems that whether through drug intoxication, religious meditation, yogic or sexual practices, carnivals, dancing, saturnalia, artistic experiences, or any of a myriad other forms of expression, every culture has found it necessary to try to escape everyday "reality" in its search for transcendence through the experience of alternate states of consciousness. This apparently universal need to seek altered states seems closely related to the search for potential space. We have seen how in the synchronized mother–infant couple a space emerges in which transitory disengagement from the system becomes possible and in which the infant begins to consolidate his own agency. It seems to be our destiny to both seek a system within which we can find self- and mutual regulation and to seek disengagement from that system so that we can emerge to find ourselves.

CHAPTER 6

Of Vampires, Ghosts, and Golems

IN THE NORMAL COURSE of development, most children experience fears of ghosts and monsters, which they handle in a variety of ways, including identifying with the monster and frightening other children in their turn. These fears arise in the earliest years, tend to peak in the oedipal phase, and are slowly mastered during latency and adolescence when the recounting of ghost stories or their contemporary equivalents becomes a counterphobic pastime. Some children, of course, never successfully integrate these fears, which remain as the substrate for a preoccupation with bizarre, fearful, and other-worldly creatures and events. The distinction between what we believe to be reality and what we believe to be fantasy is not always easy to make even for educated, mentally sound adults, as witness the controversies over unidentified flying objects and over the testimony by young children of sexual abuse, to name only two.

I have had occasion to observe a number of analysands who had an ambiguous relationship to ghosts and monsters, some of whom thought of themselves as ghostly and wraithlike while others explicitly referred to themselves as Frankensteins, golems, Draculas, and the like. While it is easy enough to believe that we all have split-off golemic tendencies, there were certain similarities among these patients that seemed to account for their greater identifications with ghosts and monsters and the ambiguous status these held between fantasy and reality.

The golem, of course, is a legend from the medieval Kabbalah, the books of Jewish mysticism, and its later form is best described by Grimm in Scholem (1965):

> After saying certain prayers and observing certain fast days, the Polish Jews make the figure of a man from clay or mud, and when they pronounce the miraculous Shemhamphoras [the name of God] over him, he must come to life. He cannot speak but he understands fairly well what is said or commanded. They call him golem and use him as a servant to do all sorts of housework. But he must never leave the house. On his forehead is written *'emeth* [truth]; every day he gains weight and becomes somewhat larger and stronger than all the others in the house, regardless of how little he was to begin with. For fear of him they therefore erase the first letter, so that nothing remains but *meth* [he is dead], whereupon he collapses and turns to clay again. But one man's golem once grew so tall, and he heedlessly let him keep on growing so long that he could no longer reach his forehead. In terror he ordered the servant to take off his boots, thinking that when he bent down he could reach his forehead. So it happened, and the first letter was successfully erased, but the whole heap of clay fell on the Jew and crushed him. [p. 159]

This form of the legend bears a strange resemblance to the tale of *Frankenstein,* written in 1818 by Mary Shelley at the age of nineteen. The theme of both is the creation of an amorphous, unformed (*Hebrew = Golem*), humanoid, manlike creature that is then imbued with life by analogy with God's creation of man.

Scholem (1965) emphasizes that Kabbalistic golem making was originally an ecstatic, mystical experience without practical purpose. It took on the pragmatic aspect of creating a demonic servant only in the sixteenth century, giving rise to the danger that he might run amok and destroy his creator and the world. But even as a mystical experience golem making was dangerous, not necessarily because of the overwhelming power of the golem but because of "the tension which the creative process arouses in the creator himself" (ibid. p. 191).

Victor Frankenstein, too, in the creation of the monster that future generations have named after him, engendered tensions that eventually caused his death. When he first animates his creation he is struck with horror at its appearance and flees, initiating a love-hate relationship in which the monster eventually kills everyone Victor loves, while Victor dies in pursuing the monster, who eventually immolates himself. But as the monster, who wants Victor to create a mate for him, beseeches (Shelley 1993 [1818]):

> "How can I move thee? Will no entreaties cause thee to turn a favourable eye upon thy creature, who implores thy goodness and compassion? Believe me, Frankenstein: I was benevolent; my soul glowed with love and humanity: but am I not alone, miserably alone? You, my creator, abhor me; what hope can I gather from your fellow-creatures, who owe me nothing?" [pp. 101–102]

and finally:

> " . . . If I cannot inspire love, I will cause fear;" [ibid. p. 154]

Thus the monster reacts to his immediate abandonment after birth by his creator, and it is unlikely to be a coincidence that Mary Shelley's mother died a few days after her birth and that the concept for the novel came to her in a half-waking nightmare. But if the theme of abandonment, loneliness, and revenge calls for our attention, the compensatory theme of merger or fusion is equally prominent. It can be no accident that generations of readers have confused the creator's name, Frankenstein, with the name of his creation, as if we were dealing with a split-off, ambivalently loved and hated part of Frankenstein's self. And it is equally interesting that one danger the golem makers courted was concretely represented by the risk of being sucked back into the very earth from which their golem was created (Scholem 1965). Thus themes of abandonment, loneliness, revenge, and fantasied reunion assert themselves, and we shall later see that a similar register is evoked by our clinical material.

But while these themes may surround the procedure of monster or golem making, it may not be entirely clear why the process of creating a humanoid is so fraught with danger and anxiety. Part of the answer may lie in the presumed hubris of competing with God. While any man and woman can together create a human and often thoughtlessly do so, only God can create one by himself, that is, noncollaboratively. And it is in this arrogant parthenogenesis, the wish to create alone, that one may find an essential element of narcissistic omnipotence and the anxieties it evokes. Interestingly, Scholem (1965) cites at least two Kabbalistic passages where God reproaches someone for studying by himself and admonishes him to seek company. In one the point is directly made:

"Are you trying to set yourself up as my equal? I am One and have created the *Book Yetsirah* and studied it: but you by yourself cannot understand it. Therefore take a companion, and meditate on it together, and you will understand it." [p. 176]

In *Frankenstein* (Shelley 1993 [1918]) too, we see the emphasis on the frightening loneliness of the singular creative act and the extent to which Victor Frankenstein, in the process of engendering his monster, has isolated himself from his friends, his family, and society:

> My cheek had grown pale with study, and my person had become emaciated with confinement . . . my eyes were insensible to the charms of nature. And the same feelings which made me neglect the scenes around me caused me also to forget those friends who were so many miles absent, and whom I had not seen for so long a time. [pp. 48–49]

And he concludes in retrospect with a warning to his listener:

> If the study to which you apply yourself has a tendency to weaken your affections, and to destroy your taste for . . . simple pleasures . . . then that study is certainly unlawful, that is to say, not befitting the human mind." [p. 49]

We can see, then, that when making a golem, a Frankenstein, or possibly other creations as well, the process is similar: one first meditates or studies at great length and in isolation; one is then caught up in a sort of hypomanic frenzy or enthusiasm where nothing else counts and there is total fixation on the goal, and, after the creation, one is assailed with fears and doubts that one has created a monster that will be shunned and should be destroyed. There are certain analogies here with post-coitum and post-partum depression.

I am surely not alone in having witnessed a similar progression amongst creative analysands who sometimes speak of their latest book, score, or sculpture as if they had created a monster that in the end is fated to destroy them. In this respect I recall a very competent young sculptor whose abilities had been neglected by her parents and subtly condemned in her first analysis as masculine, phallic, and aggressive. While she was preparing the first exhibition of her work she began to have nightmares about an aggressive man invading the office and developed fears that she was taking up too much space, would lose her boyfriend, destroy her femininity, and be abandoned by the analyst.

"People will think I'm arrogant," she said, "monstrous, swollen-headed . . . you have created a golem!" But after she had worked through the feared and degraded imagoes of both parents, she went on to make a highly successful career in a field where she had never imagined she could succeed. But lest I stray too far, let me proceed to a case vignette:

> Steven was a young professional who came to analysis because of his failing marriage and lack of interest in his work, at which he was ostensibly quite successful. But his real interests were in occult phenomena: poltergeists, werewolves, and Count Cagliostro; vampires, shamanism, altered states of consciousness, and the like. In school he had written an epistemologic paper questioning the existence of other minds. He had also experimented heavily with psychedelic drugs, but now smoked only recreationally. It soon became clear that this brilliant and successful young man experienced much of his life in a fantastic, unreal, and as-if manner. I have noted that sometimes it is those patients who feel most unreal who rely most heavily on their dreams and other altered-state phenomena, as if the most trustworthy part of themselves were to be found elsewhere, a last remnant of the true self.
>
> It also gradually emerged that his object relationships were of a peculiarly tenuous and insecure nature and that

there had been a long history of idealizations and subsequent disillusionment in many areas of his life. Indeed, the idealizations as well as the interest in occult phenomena seemed in part to be a way of restoring meaning to a world from which meaning was constantly in danger of disappearing, much as Schreber had miracled-up his world in restitution after its psychic collapse. This loss of meaning inevitably affected both object and self, so that his formerly adored wife no longer interested him, just as the position to which he had ascended after prolonged professional training no longer seemed of any worth. But what had caused Steven's world to lose meaning, if indeed it had ever been entirely meaningful, was more difficult to say.

At first we dealt with the usual narcissistic phenomena: his depleted self, his difficulties with self-regulation, his withdrawal from people and events after disappointments, his refusal to commit because then things might become real and reality would be out of his control and less than perfect. He was able to lament with evident sincerity: "My trouble is in not having an indwelling sense of self to soothe me, so the person who does that becomes more important than they should be . . . " He was even able to recognize and talk about this in the transference and live it through to some extent.

At about this time he reported a repetitive dream: *Suddenly, the horrible realization dawned on me that I had murdered someone and that I would have to spend the rest of my life covering up this fact; fleeing from it and forgetting it . . . an eternal game of running away . . .*

Over time this murder was understood in many ways: as a suicide, a patricide, a matricide, and eventually a murder of the analyst. But the initial interpretation of self-murder to keep him from committing other murders seemed to loosen things up and produce a flood of new material, among which were memories of actual attempts on the life of a younger sibling whom Steven felt had subverted his parents' attention. "Everyone thought I was the smartest one in the family and they were frightened of me, as if my intelligence might run out of control and destroy things . . . like I built a contraption with light bulbs and a lamp and bare wires and I told my brother to plug it into the wall and I intended to electrocute him . . . he did it and there were huge sparks and noises and an explosion and I was terrified. . . . Or we were astronauts and I made him get into the hamper by pretending it was a space capsule and then I closed the lid and gave him a straw to breathe through and when he was doing that I put baby powder down the straw and he started to choke and I was trying to murder him. . . . '' It is significant that these attacks, disguised as "scientific experiments," were not met with appropriate parental interventions. Shortly thereafter, as sadistic fantasies came to the fore, this patient began calling me Dr. Frankenstein and complaining that I had created a monster. But after analyzing his own "mad scientist" fears and a slightly manic episode with hypochondriasis, a period of depressive mourning ensued. Afterwards it seemed that a qualitative improvement had taken place in both his work and loving and that a person who felt half dead had begun to come alive again.

Without going into the complicated dynamics of this case, which included terrifying aggression against the joint parental image and a profound fear of destroying the object world, this vignette illustrates some of the feelings of loss, abandonment, and murderous revenge that may lead to monster fantasies. In this case the parents' ineffectual reactions toward their little scientist's acting-out both encouraged and frightened him, but often enough these fantasies incubate and flourish in a hothouse that for some reason is isolated from social influence. I have seen several instances of monster making in adults who as children were confined to bed with rheumatic fever, polio, or other long-term illnesses, as well as children who were put to bed at night with leg braces or other forms of restraint. On the one hand the child's rage and helplessness is expressed and overcompensated by these fantasies, and on the other his isolation from peer interaction removes the usual opportunities for abreaction and transformation. It may be noteworthy in this respect that Bram Stoker, the author of *Dracula,* "according to his own account . . . was very sickly during the first seven years of his life, which he spent in bed, while his mother tended him with loving care. She also entertained him with Irish ghost stories—the worst kind there is—with tales of banshees, demons, ghouls . . . " (Stade 1981, p. xi).

Dracula, incidentally, is a tale of vampirism that, although variously defined (Noll 1992), always involves the drinking of blood, whether an animal's, one's own, or another person's. The basic fantasy seems to be that blood is life giving, perhaps by its connection to the female triad of menstruation, defloration, and childbirth, and that "the primal notion that all life depends on the magic of menstrual blood . . . evolved a corresponding notion that the dead crave blood in order to make themselves live again" (Walker 1983, p. 1039). Vampires were called forth by the moon, their original Mother, who also called forth the tides and the monthly blood that made the living (Walker 1983).

In any case, it was felt that the ingestion of blood strengthens the drinker and weakens the donor, who ultimately dies or becomes a vampire himself. Exceptionally, in Catholic Communion the supply of blood is infinite, but this is because at each Mass ordinary wine is miraculously transubstantiated into Christ's blood. Perhaps one of the distinctions between the Holy Communion and its Satanic antithesis is precisely the latter's hydraulic limitation of supply as opposed to boundless Christian love. And if we consider all bodily fluids as equivalent, it is the fantasied Good Mother whose supply of milk is unlimited, but who changes into the Evil Mother when the supply is cut short.

This equation of blood and milk is supported by at

least one scene in *Dracula* (Stoker 1981 [1897]) where
the Count has finally attained his victim:

> . . . his right hand gripped her by the back of the neck,
> forcing her face down on his bosom. Her white nightdress
> was smeared with blood, and a thin stream trickled down
> the man's bare breast which was shown by his torn-open
> dress. The attitude of the two had a terrible resemblance to
> a child forcing a kitten's nose into a saucer of milk to
> compel it to drink. [p. 298]

In this scene it is Minna, the female victim, who is
being forced to drink the blood from Dracula's bosom,
an inversion of the nursing scene. But the normal desire
of the infant to suck has also been inverted to repug-
nance, just as the milk has been changed to blood and
the loving interaction into a sadomasochistic one.

Normally the milk is good and in sufficient supply,
and the satiated nursling falls asleep at the breast,
thereby completing Lewin's (1950) oral triad: to eat, to
be eaten, and to sleep. And this may be yet another
version of the merger fantasy, both in vampirism and in
the nursing situation itself, which contains the potential
to turn into vampirism from the viewpoint of both the
greedy nursling who thrives on the life-giving milk and
the suckling mother who may sometimes feel "sucked
dry" or "eaten up alive."

At this point our examination of the golem, Frankenstein, and Dracula legends has developed two themes in
common: a fantasy of good transforming into evil and a
fantasy of self transforming into other, or the reverse.
The golem, which starts as a mystical demonstration of
spiritual achievement, may end with an out-of-control
demonic servant; Frankenstein, who hoped to serve
mankind with his creation, produces an alter-ego monster who in turn wants to love but is rejected and forced

to hate; and even the vampire legend, which seems spawned in evil and sadism, can be seen to relate both to religious and maternal themes and to embody their dark sides.

If we take these fantasies to be representative of a larger class of monster, ghost, and demon fantasies, we may wonder how these themes relate to clinical material. Let me give another vignette:

Eric was a brilliant and wealthy young partner in a law firm who, despite his obvious attractiveness to women, often found himself involved in unsatisfactory relationships. He would always feel surprised when things turned sour, although there was another part of him that almost expected this to happen. When his latest girlfriend turned out to be more interested in his money than himself, he mused half-seriously: "So overnight she changed in my mind from a golden-girl into a gold-digger. . . . Could she also change into a ghost or a corpse? Could I become a monster or a Frankenstein? Would I need to become a vampire in order to get blood out of a corpse, to stay connected with her . . . ?"

At another time he reflected: "I always marvel how you come out into the waiting room and expect that it's me out there. . . . Couldn't it be someone else, another patient or a burglar . . . ? How can you be so sure that there's not a monster or the rubber plant grown all over the room waiting to grab you . . . ? Do you believe in ghosts . . . ?"

It developed that from an early age Eric had believed in ghosts and feared they were hiding under his bed. At 5 and 6 he had frightening dreams of ghosts, and later he developed fears of monsters lurking outside the house or aliens in UFOs waiting to abduct him. But at the same time he was engaged in mastering these fears by precociously immersing himself in a fantasy world of science fiction and becoming a real expert on dinosaurs and space travel.

Ghosts, of course, are revenants from another world, the dead who return to complete unfinished business. And it seemed that Eric's concern with ghosts was in part a concern with figures that had disappeared in his life: with his mother who disappeared at the time of his brother's birth and, more important, who had a habit of growing cold and disappearing emotionally whenever he disappointed her; and with his denigrated father who seemed unpredictable, looking perfectly normal at times and at other times like a monster who might kill you.

Eric himself feared his "weird experiences," a kind of negative epiphany or an abrupt transition from the good world to the bad world in which you could become anything, a Frankenstein or a monster. "Who knows what will pop up next? You never know what kind of horror is lurking inside of you waiting to come out!" In fact, in the objective world, he remained throughout a decent, loving, and loveable person, but his intense fears of object loss or inconstancy sometimes made it painful for him to maintain intimate relationships.

It is this fear of object instability, which is always correlated with a conscious or unconscious fear of self-instability, that provides the fertile spawning ground for visions of other-than-human presences. These presences may range from imaginary companions (Bach 1974), doubles, vampires, ghosts, and golems to teddy bears, security blankets, and even simpler transitional phenomena such as alternately closing one eye. The alternate closing of eyes can be not only a joyful investigation of the world but sometimes also a counterphobic defense against anxiety, an assertion that one is not passively helpless and surprised by the object's instability but can rather actively manipulate objects from stereoscopic "reality" to alternating monocular perspectives.

I recall a patient who had been a very well-brought-up little boy and who had invented not only a disreputable imaginary playmate but had also developed the visual ability to "make people go back and forth, turn them upside down, and make their faces look different." These defenses may often become pathways to mastery and sublimation, so that the creation of imaginary companions may stimulate a fertile artistic imagination or the creation of monsters may lead to a career in science fiction or psychiatry.

Of course, a principal function of other-than-human presences is to express and objectify split-off parts of the personality, albeit in another more acceptable realm, as witness the well-brought-up little boy inventing a noisy and dirty companion. Often this occurs in a family context that encourages mistrust and splitting, amidst situations that prevent the child from discussing his feelings with anyone or even admitting them to himself.

And so it happens that we see patients who, in the grip of basic or transferential mistrust, may try to do the treatment all alone, repeating the way they were obliged to do it all alone in the past. People in this auto-analytic group often bring to analysis the other-worldly presences they had conjured up to help them in childhood, for help can be had not only from friendly companions but also from evil creations who focus, condense, and displace our feelings while still expressing them, much like scapegoats. Indeed, some of these creations may contain both good and evil in emulation of their creator, as did Victor Frankenstein's monster. And, as with Frankenstein's monster, they are usually products of solitary psychic parthenogenesis.

I have mentioned the fear of hubris aroused in creating by oneself, whether a golem or a book; the anxious arrogance of noncollaboration. This may, and usually does, have multiple dynamic meanings, among which oedipal competition and triumph, sibling and preoedipal rivalry, and the pull of archaic identifications are quite common. In the higher level narcissistic disorders and perversions one often finds a collusion with the mother to preserve the dyad and evade the oedipal framework through denigrating or scotomizing the father (Chasseguet-Smirgel 1983), who may then return as a frightening nonhuman presence (Chapter 4). Also common is the concern that one's own grandiosity may get out of hand, a natural consequence in isolated children who create companions or ghosts to people their world, for their very isolation has generated anger as well as problems of control and self-regulation. And since the wish to create alone implies the figurative or literal death of everyone else, the creator may be trapped in a bind between his need for creative isolation and his need for the regulatory presence of others.

So if one function of other-than-human presences is to help objectify split-off parts of the personality, another is to aid in self and mutual regulation. We recall Eric's fear of the precariousness of his idealized objects, his anxiety lest they suddenly change: "Could she also change into a ghost or a corpse? Could I become a monster or a Frankenstein? Would I need to become a vampire in order to get blood out of a corpse, to stay connected with her . . . ?"

Here the more wraithike or emotionally unresponsive the object becomes, the more monstrous and sadistic a shape must the self assume in a desperate effort to retain the disappearing object. Conversely, when the object is experienced as an intrusive monster, the self may become a ghostly presence in evasive defense. But what Eric really needed was an object that was neither wraithlike nor intrusive, but one that would recognize and confirm all parts of himself as he experienced me doing when I so consistently expected him and no one else in the waiting room.

Finally, other-than-human presences serve an important function to ward off loneliness, as with a companion, a double, or even an occasionally friendly revenant. And when loneliness turns to despair, when all meaning seems to have fled from life, even a destructive or persecutory presence can, like Ahab's White Whale, restore a sense of purpose. Ultimately, to avoid the destruction of meaninglessness, one can become a destroyer oneself, as did Frankenstein's monster or the Marquis de Sade.

It seems that human beings are boundary-making creatures, constantly involved in distinguishing between self and other, friend and enemy, good and evil. But the boundaries are continually shifting and in need of revision and they frequently define each other so that, for example, who is one's friend may at times be a function of who is one's enemy. Moreover this need to make boundaries and erect tabus is dialectically linked with the need to transgresss or transcend them, as incest is linked with the incest tabu or the separation of human and divine linked with transcendence. It would seem that other-than-human creatures, whether monsters, aliens, ghosts, or goblins, are an inevitable product of our ever-changing psychic boundaries, for they are the exotic inhabitants of that mental territory that stretches between the self and the other, between the past and the future, between the known and the unknown.

CHAPTER 7

Being Heard: Attunement and the Growth of Psychic Structure

Exposed on the cliffs of the heart.
Look, how tiny down there, look:
the last village of words . . .
                                    Rilke

A GOOD NUMBER OF YEARS ago I began the analytic treatment of a young woman who suffered from anorexia and bulimia, complained of persistent disappointments in her love affairs, and experienced a chronic vagueness of identity that left her feeling purposeless and without desire. Although she had been in a number of previous treatments and her eating disorder and panic attacks were of serious concern, her major complaint was a feeling of emptiness, deadness, and loss of desire. She explained that she could feel alive only when passionately engaged in an affair with some idealized man, a situation which, though often repeated, seemed always to end in disaster. This syndrome is one that has by now become a commonplace of our clinical practice, but at that time it was relatively unknown to me.

Laura, my patient, was a young woman of good education and attractive appearance who maintained her weight by vomiting after eating, an action that had become almost ego syntonic for her. But what had brought her into treatment were the misfortunes of her love life. She would meet a man, become rather quickly enamored of him and pursue the relationship as much as she dared, meanwhile developing an intense fantasy life centered entirely around her loved object so that, indeed, he became the very core and essence of her being. She would think about him all the time, write him poetry, imagine where he was and what he was doing at every moment, develop an intense interest in whatever his pursuits might be, begin to live in his skin and eventually imitate him without even being aware of it. She compared herself to a chameleon, saying: "In my love for these men and especially during sex I become whatever it is that they represent for me, what I would like to be, my ideal . . . "

Sooner or later these relationships would inevitably end in disaster, and then Laura would be overcome with despair and prostrated with grief, feeling that all was lost and that her world had crumbled. Sooner or later she would pull herself together again and, after some time, begin the search anew, all the while knowing at some deeper level that she was engaged in a Sisyphean task, inherently doomed to failure.

I will not go into the dynamics of this case at any length except to confirm the obvious: that Laura was still attached to her mother in some very profound way and that, although she lived on her own and supported herself, she had never psychologically separated from the mother, whom she hated and feared from as far back as she could remember. Here, of course, the hate was conscious and the love unconscious; one finds other cases where the love is conscious and the hate unconscious. In Laura's case the relationship between the parents had been poor; the father, a somewhat remote man, was dominated by the mother and, after years of marital difficulty, they had separated when Laura was a young woman.

Although numerous attempts were made to elucidate the oedipal and preoedipal dynamics of this pathology, Laura herself had little interest in talking about anything except the succession of her affairs: their brilliant and infatuated beginnings, their precarious intermezzos, and the inevitable denouement bringing with it such pain and grief. The only other material spontaneously produced were intermittent hints of a growing and powerful attachment to me, which she acknowledged and fought against with all her strength because it seemed clear to her that this, too, would inevitably end in disaster.

In attempting to work with the material at hand, I began to ask myself the obvious but puzzling question as to why all of these failed love affairs, so passionately engaged, so earnestly pursued, and so deeply lamented had apparently not contributed in any way to some internalization or growth of psychic structure. Indeed, Laura's feelings of emptiness, loneliness, incapacity to be alone and her hunger for someone to activate her and make her feel alive seemed as strong now as they had been before any of these many relationships, in each of which she had loved intensely, lost her love object, and been deeply upset afterwards. It was as if each of these love affairs had come and gone leaving no structural internalization or nourishment behind, much as the food in her bulimic episodes was ingested and then expelled, also with little nutritive value. Why were the losses not leading to structure formation, or why were the structures not being nourished and growing, or was this a useful way to pose the question at all?

In the course of the analytic treatment, I had for some time been observing a curious symptomatic act that I had not mentioned to Laura and that she never mentioned herself. Frequently, while free associating, she would repeat an idea several times by using synonyms so that, in the end, one had the impression of listening to a human thesaurus. Thus she would say: "I was upset, disturbed, agitated, and troubled—I was all shook up." Or again: "Sometimes I feel myself stuck in, caught in, enmeshed, identified, and attached to . . . "

When eventually I inquired about this habitual behavior, she noted with pride that she had spent considerable time as a child studying the dictionary in order to perfect this ability, although she was not certain why this had begun or at what age. Speculating upon it in the hour, she offered the following possibilities, which, in retrospect, seemed to parallel the structure of the symptom she was describing:

1. "It's self-soothing . . . it just feels good for me to repeat and repeat the same word or similar words over and over again."
2. "It's a kind of greed . . . I just can't give up anything good that I want . . . like this morning I couldn't decide on which of two foods to eat for breakfast so I just ate half of each one of them . . . "
3. "It's a kind of omnipotence . . . like I've suffered so much that I should be entitled to everything—all the words in the dictionary belong to me."
4. "I should be able to figure out what the other person wants and not have him disagree and hate me . . . it pains me not to give him what he wants . . . "
5. "I give you all the words and you take what you want . . . I offer you the dictionary and if you don't like what I say you can take what you want . . . "
6. "I don't want to do the wrong thing or say the wrong word because I don't want anyone to get mad at me . . . "

That evening she had a dream: "I pictured Grand Central Station and the trains going fairly frequently . . . there was a train at 6:45 and I just made it, but then it sat there for a while but that was odd because it was only one car long . . . strange . . . not efficient . . . so many trains but each one takes so few people . . . and another at 7 and another at 7:15 . . . like the subway . . . rather than in reality trains only run every hour or two but have several cars . . . there's also something about the waiting area in the station . . . my friend Anna was there . . . for days now I've been meeting Anna and talking with her whenever I have the chance. . . . In reality, not in the dream, we got in tune yesterday, Anna and I . . . and I didn't want to break it up . . . I wanted to keep up the in-depthness . . . the in-tuneness . . . It felt so good to be completely in tune with someone . . . "

I said: "Like you never were with your mother . . . "

She began to cry. "That's when I started to study the dictionary," she said. "I thought as a kid that I must be saying something wrong. . . . If only I could say it right then she would understand how I felt. If I gave her many different possibilities, said it in many different ways, maybe one word would be the right one—maybe she would finally resonate with one word and we would be in tune for a moment.''

This immense alchemistic effort by the patient to turn herself into a thesaurus or treasury of words with the magical hope that in this way her mother might treasure *her* had never actually succeeded in reality. But the dream and her associations permitted us some insights about the meaning of the symptom, its transference reenactment, and the object-relational aspects of symbolic language.

For my own part, I began to wonder how it was that in normal development words begin to assume a meaning at all, for we know that at least with some patients words often seem to carry no emotional weight or symbolic significance—they are "just empty words"—and with others they can mean anything at all, as they did for Humpty Dumpty. And with certain patients one can sometimes discern a critical moment in their lives when words began to lose their meaning, when a regression occurred from a symbolic to a more concrete usage of words.

It seemed that the child's words must "pass through" a receptive or attuned parent and be endowed with affect and significance in the course of this passage before they return to the child as "meaningful words." That is, to paraphrase Freud, the *illumination of the* listener *must fall upon the speaker's ego* in order to impart inner life and meaning to his words. The formation of a meaning-organization (Steingart 1983) seems to require at least two people, the speaker who is "being heard" and the listener who thereby becomes a "meaning-giver." The process by which memories, perceptions, and words become integrated into a meaning-structure occurs when the emotional experience of the child is responded to by the parent—when the child feels that he is being heard. Because at this age the child and parent are joined together in a nascent meaning-organization, the parent or teacher becomes a meaning-giving object who endows the speaker's words with life, links them affectively to experience, and provides them with the deeper significance of a broadened symbolic context.

I am not, of course, describing the process by which words are learned, because for that a mere mechanical repetition might suffice to activate the child's inborn potential, but rather the process by which words become meaningful and alive because they have been differentiated and transformed by passing through the object and become in the process affect-loaded and object-cathected. That this process is reciprocal and enriches meaning for the parents as well need hardly be argued and can easily be observed watching a mother speak "baby talk" to her child.

Parents who give double-bind messages, or such deliberate assaults on the mind as *brainwashing* actually destroy the links between experience and the word, or between the thing representation and the word representation (Freud 1915b), or between the nonverbal and the verbal spheres of encoding (Bucci 1985, 1989). These decathected words then become meaningless and can be employed, as in Orwell's *1984,* for the purpose of manipulation, pseudo-communication, and double-speak, as they are by impostors and psychopaths. In such instances the meaning-giving object has become instead a meaning-destroying object.

In the case of the child or regressed adult, if the

meaning-giving object withdraws or is lost, then words may become empty and meaningless because early in life the meaningfulness of the word and of its supporting object are not experienced as separate or even as separable. Certain restitutive phenomena may then be set in motion in an attempt to remedy this loss.

With Laura, for example, her first explanation of her synonymizing was: "It's self-soothing." We can see this as a regression from the more symbolic use of object-cathected words to their more concrete employment as carriers of a magical, sensual, enactive, and masturbatory gratification.

Her second explanation: "It's a kind of greed," suggests that she is constantly hungry and that words no longer satisfy because they contain so little meaning, cathexis, or nutritive value that she needs more and more of them. Obviously, her own intense rage at her mother is also heavily implicated in this loss of the nutritive content of language; that is, words may lose meaning because the meaning-giving object withdraws, but Laura's fury at her mother also caused her to hatefully and defensively chop up, split off, poison, and expel her mother's words and her own as well. In the dream this conflict is represented by the waiting area, where Laura has been waiting for so many years to get in touch with her mother, contrasted with the manic defense of the trains that do not wait, but depart every few minutes carrying such minimal freight. There was, it seemed, a fascinating analogy between her repetitive use of empty synonyms, her repetitive consumption and expulsion of food, and her repetitive object seeking and object loss.

The third explanation: "Its a kind of omnipotence," is also restitutive in the sense that rather than being the one who is deprived of meaningful words, she becomes the manipulator of all the words in the world—a megalomaniacal synonymist who has identified with the aggressor.

If the self-soothing, greed, and omnipotence are restitutive attempts to turn impotence and passivity into power and activity, the last three explanations return once more to the originally experienced helplessness:

4. "If I can figure out what the other person wants and not have him hate me . . . "
5. "If I give you all the words (then) you can take what you want . . . "
6. "I don't want to say the wrong word because I don't want anyone to get mad at me . . . "

These seem to mean: If I do whatever you want, if I make reparation for the separation and the damage done, perhaps we can come together again in a meaning-giving organization where I can once more feel in tune with someone, as in the dream I felt in tune with my friend. I desperately wish that my mother would take care of me and be attuned to me just as I try to be attuned to my friend through synchrony and synonymy.

It may be worth noting that the repetition of words such as "in tune" and "resonate" suggest a reference to the primal musical language of mother and infant based on rhythm, melody, pitch, and timbre rather than words, that is, based on affect attunement, body ego, and nonverbal encoding rather than on symbolic content and verbal encoding.

Finally, the associations to the dream itself indicate Laura was aware that her image of very frequent trains each holding only a few people represented in some way her multitude of synonymous words, each carrying very little affect or cathexis. Combined with this was the wish that if she could meet her friend or mother in the waiting room, they might get back in tune together and she would not have to be constantly leaving, departing, escaping, and fleeing, entrained by her symptoms.

From Synonym to Metaphor

In fact, over the next few years, something very significant did happen to Laura: she remained in treatment and did not depart. And the therapeutic regression that she both longed for and struggled against eventually came about. As I became more important to her, words began to seem more significant, and there was less of a need to repeat them in multiple forms, as if sheer repetition would endow them with meaning. More and more she began to talk about herself in metaphors rather than in synonyms, and it appeared that the synonyms had served a defensive function. The regression they defended against but that she longed for finally came about, and it seemed that the struggle between synonym and metaphor had paralleled the struggle between narcissistic and object choice.

Let us listen to her again, a year later, as she describes her attempts at denial when she heard that I was going on vacation:

"When you go you lose meaning for me, you become a stranger, like I don't know you. You're unimportant, the treatment is just a process; I'm not losing you as a person but just the analysis. . . . Then I go about filling my life with other things; I don't care, you're not important, I'm a little defiant. . . . The other way I'm vulnerable and it brings up the fear . . . (Fear?) I value whatever I had that was tender and open and I'm terrified that you'll step off into some void and I'll never see you again. . . . " At this point, we were able to connect the associations about stepping off into a void with some very specific depressive memories and dreams from her childhood, at a time when Laura still loved her mother and feared for her loss. But I also began to feel that in some sense the void might represent a presymbolic void, before a potential space has been created between mother and child that would give meaning to her words and change them from empty words to words that were symbolically enriched and nutritive.

It seems that in analysis we try to reawaken through language, attunement, reconstruction, and interpretation those early affective experiences that will arouse memories of the past but put them in a new context; the earliest experiences will be recalled once again but in the context of a therapeutic object relationship (Grunes 1984). This new interaction will integrate feelings and memories of early experience, connecting the past with the present, enriching what had become empty words with a new meaning, and creating a psychic space in which meaningful interchange becomes possible. How important this felt to Laura can be seen from the following quote, in which the spatial and structural metaphors are noteworthy:

"I thought of myself as such an empty, washed-out person that you could just flush me away; so damaged that I could never be repaired. It's hard to describe what happened but I don't feel that way anymore . . . it's not being filled up, because it felt like there was nothing there to fill up. . . . It was like two halves of something coming together . . . like a container . . . and they were holding something between them . . . something that is always present and reliable and trustworthy . . . that feels like the centering and stillness that I experienced from you in the beginning . . .like some sort of faith or spiritual belief or trust or something and it's also intimately related to getting connected to my body and learning how to use it and kind of thinking and listening to my body in order to find a feeling and alignment on both a physical and a mental level also . . . to find out anything I'm not paying attention to and to be honest with myself and other people and to stop leading double lives . . . I used to feel like I had a different facade at work and another one at home and a different one with my friends and keeping track of it all was very confusing but now I'm the same person everywhere. . . . The work that I've done here with you, the work that we've done together, has filled up some space in me, some emptiness, and I know that I'll never feel that emptiness again.''

It is, of course, enormously gratifying to hear this from a patient to whom I had become very attached and who only a few years earlier had been in serious difficulty, but I thought it wise to try to understand what had transpired in theoretical terms. Perhaps the simplest explanation was that for the first time Laura had been able to relinquish those defenses against loving that she had maintained so successfully with both mother and father and that she had quite simply fallen in love with me. But why was this love being expressed in structural and spatial metaphors, and what exactly did it mean that she now felt "filled up"? Was this some sexual phantasy of possessing or becoming my baby or penis, or was I replacing some good object that had been lost at an early time and was now being refound in the transference? Was she imitating me or pleasing me as she had her previous lovers, and would the nourishment of this therapy disappear like the nutritive value of the food in her bulimia? Since our knowledge of internalization and the formation of psychic structure is still so very far from satisfactory, I thought perhaps to gain some further clues to the process by listening carefully to Laura's metaphors.

Metaphor and Action

As has often been demonstrated, metaphors are not only a product of our understanding of the world, but they in turn affect our actions so that we *behave* differently depending upon the metaphor through which we view the world (Lakoff and Johnson 1930). Thus, for example, conceiving of psychoanalysis as a *metaphoric combat,* we might be inclined to attack the defenses, expose the conflicts, break through the character armor, spy out the hidden secrets, try to ally ourselves with the stronger forces, and so forth. If, on the other hand, we conceived of psychoanalysis as a *collaborative work of art,* we might be more inclined to delineate the themes, paint the overall picture, gain a new perspective, be attuned to multimodal expressions, and emphasize the mutuality of the endeavor. Typically, each possible metaphor illuminates one aspect of the subject and obscures another: the collaborative work of art metaphor tends to obscure the conflictual nature of psychic life and therapy, while the combat metaphor tends to obscure the creative and collaborative nature of psychic life and psychotherapy. Perhaps we might mix our metaphors and think of psychoanalysis as a creative struggle of collaborative combat.

In any case, if we glance at the list of Freud's analogies in the *Standard Edition,* we are impressed once again not only with his genius and how lightly he wore his learning, but also with the variety of his metaphors, from Adam to X-ray. Nevertheless, the metaphors of psychoanalytic structural theory are generally differentiated, systematized, and organized metaphors, related to history and civilization. Thus we remember the instincts as a riderless horse, a raging river or flood, an advancing army; the ego as the rider restraining the horse or the dam or sluice-gate controlling the waters, and the superego as a non-too-benign policeman. Of course, in order to have a rider, a dam, or a policeman one must first have a social order. These metaphors all involve gestalts of forceful interaction, that is, a forceful compulsion, a potential blockage, a counter-force, and a compromise between vectors. We might call this a force and organization schema or a conflict model.

If we now think of the language employed by those analysts such as Winnicott, Balint, Kohut, Mahler, and others who speak of the *self,* we recall metaphors of symbiosis and hatching and unfolding. They speak of spaces being filled, energy stored, centers of initiative, creative potential, and new beginnings or, on the other hand, empty spaces, bottomless pits, depleted energies, and deceptive facades or basic flaws. Here the metaphors are more developmental, concerned with birth, growth, and death, and they are generally less structured, less differentiated, and more transformational. They are metaphors of negative and positive psychic states rather than of differentiated psychic structures, metaphors of growth and destructive processes rather than of drive-defense conflicts, and they describe a transformational field. We might call this a state-and-process schema, or a developmental model.

So when Laura says that she felt like "an empty, washed-out person that you could just flush away . . . so damaged that . . . there was nothing there to fill up," and that what happened was "like two halves of something coming together . . . like a container . . . and they were holding something between them . . . something that is always present and reliable and trustworthy," she might be saying that her self-experience changed from being a series of discrete, disorganized, and disconnected *states* to an integrated and meaningfully connected *self-structure* that can be counted on to be both constant and consistent within itself. When she says that "this feels like the centering and stillness that I experienced from you in the beginning . . . like some sort of faith or trust . . . and it's intimately related to getting connected to my body . . . to finding an alignment on both a physical and a mental level," she seems to imply that in some way she used my presence in the analytic situation to calm and regulate both her physical excitation and her mental ambivalence, to allow her to reconnect with her body and to feel herself whole once more. Her description of her inner experience seems to have shifted from one of a split and empty state to one of a containing structure and, interestingly enough, coincident with this change in feeling, her bulimia gradually disappeared. How can we understand this?

You may remember that for the first two years of treatment, Laura had a habit of speaking in synonyms and that it took me a long time to realize that this synonymy was part of her struggle against the therapeutic regression by denial, decathexis, and a manic use of synonyms that served the function of klang associations. That is, her use of synonyms had arisen at first as a frantic attempt to *contact* her mother, but had later become a mocking *defense* against the very contact she was seeking.

As the therapeutic regression eventually came about and I became more important to her, words also became more significant, there was less of a need to repeat them in different forms, and she began to talk about herself in metaphors rather than synonyms. One way of thinking about this was to imagine that some internal mental space that had not been reliably experienced within herself had finally been delineated or defined. This space seems best represented by a container metaphor. Since a container is defined by its boundaries, which separate the inside from the outside, her bulimia could be seen as a continual process of emptying and refilling her body container in order to redefine that space and recathect the boundaries. But what was keeping the space from being filled once and for all?

The metaphor of the body as both a container and a mental space begins to get elaborated from the oral stage onward, but the struggle about whom this container belongs to does not reach its apogee until the anal-rapprochement phase. For my patient Laura, whose experience was that her mother permitted her no viable autonomy, one possible answer to the question "Whose container am I?" was to say "If I must be your container and not my own, then I will cease to be a container entirely and I will contain nothing at all!" Thus the anorexia.

This position alternated with restitutive attempts that took the form of: "I can become a container by filling and emptying myself and controlling the process entirely by myself. Then I will be my own container and not my mother's." Thus the bulimia. Unfortunately, every time she filled herself up she would notice that some hateful part of her mother had been ingested in the process.

This struggle over who was to be whose container was the bularectic variation of the sadomasochistic object relationships that patients such as Laura usually establish and often enough reestablish within the transference. Later I shall say a word about handling the sadomasochistic transference with these patients. But first I want to emphasize that the use of bodily space in this concrete sadomasochistic fashion already suggests a developmental derailment, a failure to firmly establish a psychic space within which language can be used in a mutual dialogue to communicate, to symbolize, and to enable one to hear and to be heard (Beebe and Lachmann 1988, Brazelton, Kozlowski, and Main 1974, Stern 1985).

I believe it was precisely because this space was not reliably available that Laura employed the container of her body as a space within which to engage in sadomasochistic interactions with her mother. In other words, for patients who do not possess a safe psychic space in which dialogue can take place, bulimia and anorexia represent an abortive way of attempting to create this space in a concrete manner by transactions within their own bodies rather than within the potential space between two people. This safe internal space was what my dialogue with Laura was intended to create and reaffirm.

But perhaps at this point a word should be said about the treatment process itself. One frequently sees consultation cases in which the sadomasochistic transference has been interpreted seemingly to no avail, or in which it has been jointly acted out in ongoing squabbles about who is going to control whom until both parties to the analysis have reached a state of mutual exasperation and exhaustion. In many such cases the analyst seems not to have fully appreciated that the patient's mental organization is in some respects still somewhat undeveloped, and this regardless of the patient's intelligence or worldly achievements. If we remember Laura's change from the use of concrete synonyms to the gradual employment of metaphors, we might say that you cannot explicate the transference, which is a metaphor, to a patient who has difficulty dealing with symbols and metaphors. These are Freud's "soup and dumpling" patients whose mental organization, at least in the transference regression, is unable to accommodate the symbolism of transference metaphor. What this means in practice is that such patients will confuse or confabulate what should be transferential and symbolic issues into *real* issues of love or death and will struggle with the analyst as if the analyst were *in fact* trying to rape or kill them.

Laura, whose real mother would not allow her free access to the refrigerator, stole food from my garbage can; because her real mother would not allow her into the living room, she came late to avoid dirtying my waiting room and then managed to spill food and drink over everything. My clinical sense was that in the first phase of treatment these enactments should not be interpreted, because interpretation would have been humiliating and would have renewed the sadomasochistic struggle, and what was needed was simply a safe place to be.

I felt that with Laura the symbolizing functions had either not been firmly established or had regressed and that interpretations that might have been accepted or rejected out of transference love or hate would have as little effect on structure building as had her previous affairs. By this time it had become clear to me that even her verbal synonymy was a kind of verbalized acting out or, more properly, enactment.

It seemed imperative that she be helped to create some personal psychic space in which her own volition, effectance, and continuity could be vitally experienced. This space, which in healthy people is created symbolically when they speak and expect to be heard could be created for Laura only by symbolic enactment within a living analytic space.

And so when Laura learned that I was not going to struggle with her about who controlled the waiting room, the garbage can, her mental contents, or the treatment, but that I was clear about not letting myself be unreasonably imposed upon, she could begin to construct a psychic space, free of the fear of being invaded or of invading me. And within this space something symbolic could begin to grow between us.

One of the things that began to grow was her ability to use metaphor instead of synonymy. With synonymy or similarity she could be just like me, or try to please me or to merge with me, but metaphor required a more differentiated and objective perspective and the ability to shift perspectives, that is, to understand that the same fact could be seen from different points of view and mean different things to different people (Bach 1985, DeLoache 1987). Not that Laura hadn't employed some metaphor before the treatment, but it was primarily the body as metaphor, the concreteness of the body used to represent feelings and ideas that she could not mentally entertain. Now that she had a mental space of her own she could begin to use mental metaphors instead of bodily ones because she felt as if her mind belonged to her and was capable of communicating interactively with other minds.

In cases such as this I feel that a considerable period of holding or attunement, which is *not* the same as passivity, mirroring, corrective emotional experience, or role playing, may be necessary in order to provide the patient with the psychic space I have tried to describe.[1] If the patient is persistently confronted with

---

[1] It may be useful to attempt a preliminary distinction between attunement and empathy. Empathy implies a sharing and receptivity to another person's expressed thoughts and feelings; the identification of one ego with another. Attunement implies a receptivity to another's not-yet-verbalized wishes through resonance and harmony with his rhythms, gestures, sounds, and affect; interventions deal primarily with proprioceptive, kinaesthetic, tactile, and somatosensory experiences. Attunement is linked to early affect-motor states and the early body-ego and is frequently nonverbal. Although words may be used to express both empathy and attunement, empathy emphasizes their symbolic content whereas attunement emphasizes their form and function, as in the caretaker's "baby-

the analyst's reality before this psychic space has developed, then two common miscarriages of analysis may ensue. In the first the patient becomes acquiescent and agrees, but does not develop a genuine sense of self and a prolonged pseudo-analysis results. In the second the patient disagrees and eventually either acts out or conforms, but becomes internally isolated, suspicious, and schizoid. He learns, in short, to keep his thoughts to himself and develops the conviction that there is no one in the world he can really trust and nothing to believe in. Fortunately, in the case I am describing, Laura learned both to love and to separate.

On Being Heard and Multiple Worlds

Just as self-recognition in the mirror serves as an important landmark in the development of self-awareness, so the experience of being heard may serve as a landmark in the formation of symbolic meaning both developmentally and in therapeutic analysis. The attunement of another person to one's inner emotional state and the resulting feeling of consonance and cohesion between inner experience and outward expression makes for an early experience of trust and the creation of a psychic space that seems necessary for healthy structuralization to occur. Only upon the solidity of this primary coherent foundation do the later losses, disillusionments, and events such as the first lie become developmentally healthy steps.

---

talk." The attuned person anticipates, "holds," and regulates these early affect-motor states, thus placing them in a context that promotes self- and mutual regulation, self-differentiation, and structure formation (e.g., Stern 1985). One might say that attunement is the method for transforming Winnicott's potential space into Freud's ego space.

When this affective foundation is not firmly in place, the child, and later the adult, remains forever doubtful about the reality of his inner experience. Although one may repeatedly reassure him that his thoughts and emotions are natural or acceptable, this simply does not feel the same as having had another person attuned to his affective state. *For we assume that what is first laid down and psychically represented in infancy are affect states and affect cycles and that the deepest levels of meaningfulness resonate with these affect states.* In analysis we must show the patient not only that we have heard what he said and that we understand what it means, but above all that we are able to share his feeling about it. For this to happen it is important that the patient be listened to in an open, nonstereotyped way.

For a person to feel heard, he must know that he is not just being reflected, which could be done by a mirror, or imitated, which could be done by a tape recorder. He must know that his words have passed through a living human being who understands them, who holds and contains them, *including their disavowed portions,* and who transforms them and reflects them back in a way that is distinctive for each listener and recognizes the speaker's uniqueness. Thus the speaker's words are returned to him, restored by having passed through and been responded to by the listener, and they are returned to him in many modalities, within a broadened context that captures his feelings and yet somehow also enriches and illuminates them. *In this way the child first begins to learn that the same reality can be viewed in different ways by the same person or by different people at different times.*

Of course, in the baby's post-omnipotent state, when attunement can no longer be complete and symbolic language has become critical, there must also be recognition of the inevitable tension that arises when one separate agent attempts to communicate with another separate agent through periods of presence and absence, of disjunction and dissonance. The post-omnipotent child must learn that the listening mother has to make an effort to understand him because in fact they do not speak identical languages. For the *mother of separation* must communicate empathy and understanding within the context of a sense of difference, and this is what makes dialogue with a living human being so absolutely unique. When it succeeds, the speaker is confirmed in his sense that his feelings are real and that it is possible for another, separate human being to share them. When the understanding is attained that one's own point of view and another's point of view can both have reality and legitimacy, then effective interpretation, and particularly transference interpretation, becomes possible.

But I should also emphasize that, through being heard, the child learns how to listen and learns that he too can hear his mother, be attuned to her, and comfort *her*. He learns the very important lesson that his words can *have an effect* and that they can either bring him solace or give solace if necessary. That is, he learns that other points of view exist and can influence him and that he can influence them. He discovers, through mutual identificatory processes, that his mother can understand him and he can understand her through the sharing of comparable inner experiences.

Thus it would seem that a person's sense of self is intimately tied to being experienced as vital and alive by another human being. While this may seem obvious when we think about infants and their mothers, the experiments on sensory isolation and stimulus deprivation, as well as reports of brainwashing and solitary confinement, all demonstrate that even the healthiest of us needs some ongoing, continual input or nourishment to adequately maintain our sense of self.

It appears that each human being is constantly constructing his own personal world and continuously checking it for coherence, consistency, and validity. We have all experienced anxiety at the boundaries of our personal worlds, in altered states of consciousness, at traumatic moments of crisis, or when traveling in a totally foreign culture. Although each of us has his own personal world, normally these all belong to and are consistent with some larger contextual world or realm of discourse. In this sense we might say that certain patients have never constructed a world at all, or have deconstructed or lost the meaning of their worlds, and that one function of the analyst is to help them construct their own version of reality or to help them refind that world in which their version of reality makes sense. And it seems clear that one of our principal measures in this endeavor is to *become that kind of listener* who can give meaning to the world that the patient is working to construct.

CHAPTER 8

On Omnipotence and Disillusionment

AS THE WIDENING SCOPE of psychoanalysis brings more and more difficult patients under the analyst's purview, it becomes clear that the issue of omnipotence is a major problem in the treatment of the narcissistic, borderline, and psychosomatic conditions and the resolution of the sadomasochistic and omnipotent transferences they tend to evoke.

On a number of occasions Freud commented on the fact that psychoanalysis was the last of three great blows to man's "naive self-love" or "craving for grandiosity" or what we might call omnipotence. The first or cosmological blow was when Copernicus realized that our earth was not the center of the universe; the second or biological blow was when Darwin demonstrated that we do not have a privileged position among the earth's inhabitants, and the third, or psychological blow, was when Freud showed that our ego is not even master in its own house. With the first we seem to have lost our preeminent place in the universe, with the second we seem to have lost our divine origins, and with the third we appear to have lost control even over our own minds. It is worth noting the sequence in which these discoveries were made, for it seems to have been easier to achieve an objective viewpoint about ourselves the farther away that objectivity resided from the center of our own narcissism.

The "classical" view, as enunciated by Ferenczi in his paper, "Stages in the Development of the Sense of Reality" (1913), recapitulates this presumed history of mankind in the development of each human being. In this view the innate omnipotence of the child is slowly tempered as he repeatedly discovers that he is not the center of the universe nor the absolute master of his destiny, leading to a gradual though incomplete replacement of the pleasure principle by the reality principle.

Over the last several decades, Balint (1968), Kohut (1971), Winnicott (1965), and others have presented accounts that some have taken to mean the obverse, namely, that defects in early parenting may in fact produce omnipotence as a way of handling feelings of helplessness and annihilation. Novick and Novick (1991) have neatly summarized this: "The classical view is that failure of omnipotence forces the child to turn to reality, but we believe that it is the failure of reality which forces the child to turn to omnipotence" (p. 320).

Some part of this apparent disagreement may hinge on our definition of omnipotence, a term used in many different ways. Let me begin with one meaning centered around the acute sense of self-as-being or existing, the idea of psychobiological aliveness or libidinization, Winnicott's I AM (1965). This is the foundation for what I call subjective self-awareness, experiencing oneself as the center of actions, feelings, and thoughts. The establishment of this vital sense begins early in life, as we know from Spitz's hospitalized infants (Spitz 1945,

1946), who received little emotional care and developed marasmus, a state of apathy, withdrawal, and physical deterioration that is the extreme opposite of psychobiological aliveness. This marasmus-like lack of libidinization may sometimes be found in severely deprived patients who present with anorexia, bulimia, delicate self-cutting, or other self-mutilating symptoms. An extraordinary literary example can be found in the novel *Perfume* (Suskind 1986), about a delibidinized infant who becomes a monster and murders beautiful women in order to capture from them their sense of aliveness and libidinization that he felt deprived of through lack of early mothering (see Chapter 4).

In any case, this extreme sense of libidinized being and aliveness, the feeling I AM, is one usage that I call *psychobiological omnipotence.* Its development has been investigated by Freud (1914b), by Lacan (1949) in his theory of the mirror stage, and by Stern (1985) in his theory of the core self, to name only a few. At 8 months the infant joyfully recognizes the connection between his own experienced movements and their reflection in the mirror image. This "jubilant assumption of his specular image" (Lacan 1949) marks a moment of Gestalt cohesion and grandiose omnipotence that is a "high" of psychobiological aliveness and subjective self-awareness, later to be repeated and transformed in the practicing period and again in adolescence. But it already carries within it the paradox of the human existential dilemma, for within a year the child not only feels that the image is subjectively himself, but he also begins to understand that he can become the object of his own and someone else's scrutiny from the outside, like an alienated thing. As Amsterdam and Levitt (1980) report:

In the first year of life, infants responded to their mirror images with unrestrained enthusiasm and delight. In the second year of life, children no longer respond to the mirror with naive joy, but they withdraw and become wary of their images. Self-conscious behavior follows and continues through the period when children show objective recognition of the image starting at 18 months. [p. 68]

One might say that the child has eaten of the Tree of Knowledge and in the process has acquired the ability to become ashamed of himself. And indeed it is only after this rudimentary acquisition of objective self-awareness that a second type of reactive omnipotence can occur, that is, a *defensive omnipotence* as a reaction to unbearable feelings of shame, humiliation, and death of the self. Thus, when Bornstein (1949) told Frankie that his treatment was coming to an end, he reacted with the fantasy that he was the omnipotent King Boo-Boo, a fantasy that Winnicott (1966) saw as a repetition of his reaction to the original traumatic abandonment by his mother. Dynamically, we understand this to mean: "No! I am not a helpless dependent child at the mercy of adults who abandon me. On the contrary, I am an omnipotent king and can do whatever I want and have power over everyone else."

Another well-known example might be Schreber's omnipotent reactions to the deprivations and humiliations imposed by his father. It is worth noting that in both cases these fantasies of omnipotence are compensatory reactions for underlying feelings of impotence, humiliation, and despair, that is, a manic defense.

A third kind of omnipotence might be called cognitive or *developmental omnipotence*. For just as man once viewed himself as the center of the universe, in some ways the young child still views himself as the primary center of feelings, thoughts, and orientation. Piaget and others have studied the transformations of this kind of egocentrism and the developmental growth of such basic reality concepts as object permanence, space, time, and causality (Michotte 1963, Piaget 1954). Indeed, Piaget has spoken of this development as a move toward decentration, that is, a move toward not centering the world exclusively around the self. For example, children ages 4 to 6 are generally incapable of picturing how an object might look from the viewpoint of a differently situated observer, and they maintain that it would look the same as it does from their own viewpoint (Piaget and Inhelder 1956). But even after they lose this developmental omnipotence and gain the ability to imagine a change of viewpoints, this incremental gain in objective awareness of the world may or may not be reflected in their objective awareness of themselves.

I hope to have clarified certain usages of *omnipotence,* as well as the inherent tensions that exist between subjective self-awareness, with its potential for aliveness and psychobiological omnipotence, and objective self-awareness, with its potential for self-knowledge, shame, and defensive omnipotence. The dialectic between these two types of awareness is basic to the human mind (Auerbach 1990, 1993, Bach 1980, 1985), and problems with the smooth integration of these two perspectives are characteristic of narcissism. Narcissistic personalities try to solve the dilemma and eliminate the dialectic by eliminating one of the two perspectives and living either in self-omnipotence (overinflated narcissist with grandiose and sadistic fantasies) or in other-omnipotence (deflated narcissist with merging and masochistic fantasies.) These questions of dependence–independence and separation–merger become important when we look to the empirical research bearing on issues of omnipotence.

In the last two decades an explosion of fascinating infant research has demonstrated hitherto unsuspected perceptual, memorial, and discriminatory capacities in the very young child in the alert waking state of consciousness (Emde 1983, 1988, Lachmann and Beebe 1992, Lichtenberg 1983). Although this alert waking state represents a small part of the neonate's day, it nevertheless suggests that rudimentary capacities for self–other discrimination exist perhaps from birth. This has led to a reconsideration of concepts such as autism, merger, and symbiosis (Lachmann and Beebe 1992, Stern 1985), as well as clarification of the difference between fusion and undifferentiation when applied to the mother–infant couple (Auerbach 1993). While it is important to reemphasize that the neonate is programmed from birth for object relating, it is also important to remember that the infant is in a state of psychobiological dependence for a very long time, a dependence that may be crucial for the development of structure and character (James 1960, Winnicott 1965).

Although the neonate seems able to discriminate self and other when in alert states, he might not always be motivated to do so and in fact it may be harmful for optimal development if this discrimination is made too sharply, too early, or for too long (Ellman 1992). In the early weeks the infant spends much of his time asleep or in nonalert states and "we have almost no evidence about the infant's capacity to take in external stimulation or to engage in any of the perceptual processes during the high activation states of distressful hunger or the very low activation states of somnolent satiation" (Stern 1985, p. 237).

Ultimately, it seems amusing that we have all once

been infants but are unable to recall this and, despite the richness of our clinical observations and theory, we are obliged to fill in the gaps in our knowledge with fantasy. Historically, many analysts have chosen to view the earliest months of development through the metaphor of symbiosis, which emphasizes the infant's psychobiological undifferentiation and the sense that all the infant's wants are met without his need or even his ability to know this is happening. One might view this as a powerful adult fantasy of symbiosis or oneness, retroprojected onto the infant.

Under the sway of the last two decades of research emphasizing the infant's capacities, another metaphor has emerged reminiscent of Ferenczi's (1933) fantasy of The Wise Baby. This is a fantasy of an infant who is prematurely cognitive, intelligent, and can speak at birth. But as Ferenczi and Winnicott have noted, the infant becomes cognitive and develops a precocious ego as overcompensation for early trauma to his dependence. So the first fantasy is of a dependent infant, lost in his subjectivity, whereas the second is of an independent infant, objectively self-aware. The powerful impact that these fantasies have on our scientific discussions only illustrates once again how difficult it is to grapple with the paradoxical limitations on our awareness.

Nevertheless, those who work with disturbed patients suffering from early trauma and lacking basic trust are of necessity interested in states of clinical dependence. Winnicott was one of these, and he imagines normal development as starting with absolute dependence in which "the infant has no means of knowing about the maternal care . . . Under favorable conditions the infant establishes a continuity of existence and then begins to develop the sophistications which make it possible for impingements to be gathered into the area of omnipotence" (1965, pp. 46–47). Here Winnicot is developing yet another meaning for omnipotence, not only as a nondefensive experience of magical control but also as an experience of creating and re-creating the gratifying object, which, with that object's compliance, leads to its becoming objectively perceived. "At this early stage the facilitating environment is giving the infant the experience of omnipotence. . . . The infant experiencing omnipotence under the aegis of the facilitating environment *creates and re-creates the object,* and the process gradually becomes built in, and gathers a memory backing" (Winnicott 1965, p. 180). I take it that Loewald is referring to similar processes when he states that " . . . through interaction within the mother–child psychic field . . . Phenomena such as instincts and objects gradually become constituted, by differentiation and integration, in those interaction processes" (Loewald 1980, p. 129). And infant research is increasingly demonstrating the precise mechanisms, such as simultaneous vocalization (Stern 1983), affect attunement (Stern 1985), and match, mismatch, and repair (Lachmann and Beebe 1989), which may create not only experiences of togetherness, oneness, and omnipotence but may also lead to increasingly differentiated self- and object representations.

It is these *experiences of omnipotence* in the phase of absolute dependence that constitute part of the foundation on which trust in oneself and in the world is built. Indeed, it is when these *experiences of omnipotence* are lacking and the object's failures impinge on the child that a reactive *defensive omnipotence* arises to deny and overcompensate for feelings of annihilation and death of the self.

Winnicott, in his poetic fashion, is proposing a developmental line for the establishment of basic trust, starting with the infant's experiences of omnipotence and including the creation of potential space, transitional space, playing, creativity, and the cultural milieu. By implication, Klein's paranoid-schizoid position signals a failure in this developmental line in the area of the early experience of omnipotence (Ellman 1992). Winnicott is also proposing a therapeutic reworking of this failure, starting with the holding environment in which "the traumatic factor enters the psycho-analytic material in the patient's own way, and within the patient's omnipotence" (1965, p. 37), and proceeding from there by a process of optimal disillusionment.

I believe that basic trust grows out of such experiences of omnipotence tempered by optimal disillusionment, or optimal match, mismatch, and repair. The infant's ability to discriminate self and other in the alert waking state of consciousness may well coexist with experiences of togetherness, oneness, and omnipotence in other states of consciousness (Pine 1986), just as in adults these same discriminations vary with states of consciousness (see Chapter 5). Such experiences of omnipotence, far from implying unrelatedness, can only arise in the context of exquisitely sensitive interactions between mother and infant. Cumulative gross mismatches between mother and infant will in fact destroy experiences of omnipotence and trust, force premature discriminations of self and other, internalize expectations of interactive misregulation and lead ultimately to defensive omnipotence.

One might imagine a developmental line for subjective self-awareness, the sense of oneself as the center of action, feeling, and thought, that starts from psychobiological omnipotence and includes notable transformations in Lacan's mirror stage, the practicing subphase, and in adolescence. In adults one notes subjective self-awareness in the athlete at peak performance or the artist at moments of creation, all totally absorbed in themselves. Indeed, research with adults (Duval and Wicklund 1972) has confirmed what our clinical observations suggest: that in this state people tend to feel happier and tend to *over*estimate their own powers.

The complement to this state is objective self-awareness in which one is acutely aware of oneself and one's thoughts, feelings, and actions as simply one object among others, one self among other selves. The developmental line for objective self-awareness may begin with infantile precursors of shame (Tomkins 1963) or of interpersonal inefficacy (Broucek 1991) and includes self-recognition in the mirror at 18 months and later transformations during rapprochement, in the post-oedipal period, in late adolescence, and even in adulthood (Auerbach 1993). We observe objective self-awareness in the rapprochement child who suddenly becomes aware of his vulnerabilities and his need for mother, or in the artist or scientist who presents his work to a jury of peers. Objective self-awareness carries with it a large potential for shame and guilt, and in fact Duval and Wicklund's (1972) research has demonstrated that in this state people tend to become more depressed and to *under*estimate their own powers.

I have tried to show that there is normally a constant dialectic tension between these two states: subjective self-awareness is important to maintain our sense of wholeness and aliveness and increase our self-esteem, whereas objective self-awareness is important to maintain our sense of proportion and belongingness and to modulate our self-esteem. Defects of subjective self-awareness are associated with conditions like false self and as-if personality, whereas defects of objective self-awareness are associated with conditions in which grandiosity and omnipotence prevail. More commonly, people have difficulties modulating, integrating, and appropriately switching between both perspectives. And it is perhaps in the transitional area between mother and infant, between fantasy and reality, that such modulations and integrations first begin. But let me now turn to more directly clinical considerations.

I will make a distinction between two levels of reactive omnipotence that are clinically discernible, although they sometimes appear in admixtures or at different stages of treatment. The first level results from a failed stage of absolute dependence and is analagous to Klein's paranoid-schizoid position. This is a pre-rapprochement pathology, often with a paranoid tinge, and it sometimes evokes an omnipotent transference. A common example of this is the patient who either will not allow the analyst to talk or who will not himself talk for extended periods of time, such as Kent in Chapter 3. Here safety is achieved at the expense of a two-person psychology and there is no real dialogue, not even of a sadomasochistic kind. Some of these patients are exquisitely attuned to the inanimate environment, which they animate in a paranoid way, and they may be obliged to control time, distance, sound, odor, and other dimensions of the analytic space in order to preserve their safety.

This early level of omnipotence is difficult to work with and at first the analyst allows for rhythmicities of self- and mutual regulation to occur so that eventually a free space may develop in which the patient can feel safe and regulated (see Chapters 3 and 5). The analyst remains both attuned and synchronized not only in intellectual but primarily in sensual modalities such as rhythm, breathing, and so forth. Often female analysts report that their menses tend to synchronize with their female patients' or vice versa, since at this stage all operations are reversible.

Paradoxically, this earlier stage omnipotence is intensely concerned with retaining the analyst as an omnipotent "object," since for these patients to take away their omnipotence in analysis is to lose their object. Obviously, this occurs anyway in progressive cycles of attachment, destruction of self and object, and survival of self and object. At each stage analytic trust is lost and hopefully refound and reconfirmed (Ellman 1991). Dosage is all-important and depends on our reasonable control of the countertransference, which is made easier if we bear in mind our goal of allowing for the development of an open space within a mutually regulated environment.

The second level of omnipotence with which I am primarily concerned here is an anal-rapprochement pathology where a self and other are reasonably demarcated, although the focus of importance, power, and libidinal attachment may shift back and forth between the two. Here the patient wants something from the other, usually in a sadomasochistic way. Thus his fears are not about an objectless world, but rather about the shifting allocations of power and libidinal attachment between self and other. Let me give some examples:

> A very successful professional woman yearned for promotion to a more prestigious position. She had repeatedly spoken to her boss who had repeatedly assured her that he wanted to promote her but that, for reasons he explained at length, he was unable to do so at the present time. Although she was confident of her boss's good will, which had been evidenced in many other ways, she refused to believe that he *couldn't* give her the promotion and

instead insisted that he *wouldn't* give it to her. "If he loved me enough," she said, "he would find a way."

Both the patient and her boss were temporarily helpless in this situation, but she had endowed him with her "omnipotence by proxy." This turned out to replicate the way her mother had used the patient as a narcissistic object, for when the child complained that she couldn't control herself the mother would respond: "If you loved me enough you would do it for me . . . "

Another case was brought to me by a colleague who had been treating a disturbed young man for many years. In the course of that treatment this man, who came from symbiotic alcoholic parents, had managed to leave home, get a profession, and become quite successful and independent, with a lively social life. The treatment was an undoubted success until termination came into view, at which point the patient would consistently regress, get drunk, act out, and do everything possible to destroy the gains he had made. Having analyzed the masochistic components for a long time with only partial success, my colleague came for a consultation. After a while I was able to point out that the patient maintained a sadomasochistic situation by deliberately keeping the analysis in a see-saw state with either the analyst omnipotent and the patient needy and helpless, or the patient omnipotent (through intoxication or destructive enactments) and the analyst helpless. The point was to keep *somebody* omnipotent and *somebody* helpless in order to avoid the more frightening situation of equality between two collaborators. A situation of equality was dreaded because it meant that both participants were limited, that the therapy was limited and imperfect, that it would come to an end, and that ultimately each participant would die. This patient was ready to sacrifice his treatment and his hard-won career if need be in order to hold on to the illusory omnipotence he experienced in the painful but familiar merger with the archaic imagoes of his alcoholic and symbiotic parents.

I hope it becomes clear in these illustrations that the patient's omnipotence can survive equally well in an introjected or projected form and that these two are functionally interchangeable. Of course, for some people belief in the inevitable triumph of a social, political, or religious cause can also serve as omnipotence by proxy. It may be that historically it was easier for people to deal with their strivings for perfection and omnipotence at a time when most people believed in God, a time when every artisan was accustomed to leave a tiny but visible defect in his work because "only God makes perfect things."

Indeed, in our culture of disbelief it seems difficult even to understand that men might once have taken joy at the thought of their own death, because death to the believer is a transcendence or joining with the omnipotent, whereas to a nonbeliever it is the ultimate limitation on his power. Our culture has solved the problem of disbelief largely by denying the inevitability of death, which may have led to an increase in problems of narcissism and omnipotence or at least a change in their modes of expression.

In any case the subject of death rarely seems to arise in many analyses unless there has been a past trauma or an intercurrent illness or actual death. But if attention is paid it may often be seen to emerge in the termination phase, when fantasies of rebirth as well as of death and other limitations on omnipotence naturally come to the fore.

In general, people seem less afraid of death if they can look back on a well-lived life. But in any case it is difficult to imagine our own death until it is definitively situated in time. Beckett makes this point beautifully in his essay on Proust. Speaking of Swann, he says: "His indifference at parting from Albertine . . . is transformed into the most horrible anxiety by a simple remark addressed by her to her aunt or friend: 'Tomorrow, then, at half-past eight.' The tacit understanding that the future can be controlled is destroyed. The future event cannot be focussed, its implications cannot be seized, until it is definitely situated and a date assigned to it" (Beckett 1965, 1987, p. 16).

Similarly, we see many patients who are more or less out of touch with their anxieties about termination or other limitations until a date has been definitely fixed, at which time their tacit omnipotence is pricked. They have made an appointment in Samara that cannot be broken.

One might also argue that a person cannot truly be afraid of death until he knows the date, which fits with Freud's assertion that there is no fear of death in the Unconscious. Often fears of death turn out really to be fears of a *living death,* that is, of having once been or of still being dead while yet alive. It appears that what many people experience as a fear of death is actually a fear of "death of the self" (Bach 1985), that is, an experience of such a massive shock to their childhood omnipotence that it made them feel dead or as if an important part of themselves had died (Ferenczi 1988). It is this fear, retroactively experienced, that often passes for fear of death. This is related to Freud's notion of the kernel of reality in psychosis, or Winnicott's idea that fear of going mad is often fear of returning to a childhood psychotic state *that had already occurred.*

I had long fantasied that a scientific test for progress in the treatment of defensive omnipotence might be to introduce a standardized narcissistic insult at intervals throughout the treatment, but this seemed unfeasible for humanitarian reasons. Not long ago a colleague told me about a similar experiment in nature, when at several intervals over the years she had experienced such a deafening drilling over her office that she and her patient were able to hear each other only with the greatest difficulty.

On the first occasion the patient insisted that the analyst should make the drilling stop, protested that the analyst wasn't protecting her or providing a safe space, that she was allowing others to intrude on the treatment, and, finally, that if the analyst really loved her she would find a way to silence the noise. In the end the patient began to scream that if it were *her* office she would certainly stop the noise, reassuming out of desperation the projected omnipotence.

Some years later when the same situation recurred, the patient came in, listened for a few minutes, stated that "this is impossible and could we reschedule the hour?" and then left, after noting that it must also be difficult for the analyst and perhaps she could use the remainder of the hour to take a walk outside.

In this example the omnipotence, which at its height had gotten tossed back and forth like a hot potato, had by now become reasonably well integrated into self-esteem and regard for others.

In some cases, one can watch the shift of idealized omnipotence from the other onto the self, with frightening or embarrassing results:

A woman who had grown up in a chauvinistic family totally idealizing her father once remarked: "I must have been defending against some enormous ambitions when I attached myself to Daddy and worshipped him and got my power through him by proxy. Because if I even allow myself to imagine that I can have it myself then I start to get intense and grandiose and I want to be extraordinary and a genius and I'm embarrassed to even tell you what I'm thinking . . . I guess now that I've given up idealizing my father I really want to be a female version of the way I saw my daddy when I was a little girl. . . . "

It should be emphasized that when an idealized omnipotent figure is given up and the power is not simply displaced to someone else but is assumed by the patient, then this experience can become terribly frightening as the split-off aspects emerge. Patients frequently have dreams or fantasies of being werewolves, monsters, vampires, or demons, and they are only too happy to have this analyzed simply as talion for the destruction of their former idol rather than also face their terror at the omnipotence of their own growing powers.

Often one finds an intricate complex of developmental and defensive omnipotence that has grown over time, particularly in cases where the parents have denied important aspects of reality or where cultural differences force the child to negotiate between two very disparate worlds.

> Early in her analysis Elizabeth, an unmarried young woman, mentioned that she saw auras around certain people and that she had interviewed several analysts and decided to begin treatment with me because of my positive aura. It took more than a year for us to understand what this meant. At some point in the treatment she began to notice books and furnishings in my office that she hadn't seen before and very tentatively began to comment on them. I gradually discovered that growing up in a hypocritical and physically abusive household, she had been systematically taught not to notice many things and especially not to comment on them. When she noticed that her mother, who preached honesty, was cheating, or that her father, who preached schooling, rarely read a book, she was rebuked and beaten unmercifully. Thus she learned not to notice, but the stimuli that she didn't notice were nevertheless registered, eventually to emerge in other modalities as an "aura" composed of light, color, and tactile sensations. This aura, in effect, conveyed to her in other modalities very much the same conclusions she

might have arrived at had she been "allowed" to notice and observe me in the context of my books and furnishings.

Although Elizabeth was a quite extraordinarily intelligent, sensitive, and aware person, her ability to observe and appreciate herself, her objective self-awareness, seemed to fail her at times. This was in part because of her parents' failure to reflect her objectively as, for example, by denying and discounting what she actually saw. She felt despairing and humiliated about her abused childhood, and one of the many small ways she used to reassert her potency and self-esteem was via the auras. The dynamic meaning was: "No! It's not that I'm forbidden to see what everyone else can see. On the contrary, I am able to see what no one else can see!"

In this example the cognitive and the dynamic are enmeshed. Elizabeth's difficulty in seeing herself objectively (developmental omnipotence) was in some part the result of her parents' failure to reflect her objectively. But it had also become infused with elements of rage, denial, idealization, and manic defense so that she alternated between sometimes feeling herself the worst in the world and sometimes the best—powerless and humiliated but also omnipotent.

It was this reactive omnipotence that presented the greatest therapeutic difficulty because it involved sado-masochistic fantasies of power and transcendence through self-destructive acting-out. One prominent factor in these enactments was the unconscious need to remain tied to powerful parental imagoes. Being at one with her parents evoked painfully familiar feelings of humiliation but also of masochistic attachment to an omnipotent figure: omnipotence by proxy. When, in the course of treatment, she could instead experience despair at her parents' failures and allow herself closeness in a benign, nonhumiliating situation, then this aspect of the need for painful and self-destructive enactments slowly disappeared.

And indeed, defensive omnipotence seems to result largely from the denial of an early disappointment or disillusionment, some experience or cumulative trauma that left the child in a state of utter unredeemable despair. This is precisely the kind of despair that Ferenczi has written about so movingly in his *Clinical Diary* (1988), a despair so unbearable that it is quickly covered by denial. Here is a brief example of despair precipitated by a psychophysical trauma:

> Carl was raised by a mother who, as it gradually emerged in the analysis, seemed either to overwhelm him completely or else to disappear entirely. We could verify even to this day that she would bombard him with meaningless words, change the subject when she got anxious, and then emotionally vanish. When the patient was not quite three a baby brother was born and shortly thereafter Carl was sent to nursery school. The idea of leaving mother alone with baby brother seemed intolerable. He came down with a cold that turned into bronchial pneumonia.
>
> Carl remembers the doctor and his mother discussing this, and then he was whisked away and put in an oxygen tent. He felt betrayed at the way he was taken without a word and put in this plastic dome. He never went back to school that year. He lay in the bubble and he learned to tell time by watching the clock and waiting for his mother to arrive. It seemed that she was always late, always busy with his brother. He felt abandoned and betrayed and he came out of the hospital vowing that never again would he allow himself to need anything from anyone. Even as an adult he would still retreat to some version of the bubble to protect himself and preserve his life. His outward demeanor was cold, sanitized, and unreachable, as if in his omnipotent bubble he could deny both life and the "death

of the self" that he had once experienced. But when threatened Carl would freeze like a frightened animal and become passively masochistic, as if the death he feared had already occurred.

This denial of the "death of the self" usually includes a denial of death itself and especially of the passive longings for death that such an experience engenders. These passive longings may be handled as Carl did or they may be split off and experienced in a depersonalized and masochistic way as fascination: "I was fascinated with the idea of just walking into the water"; "There was an impulse to throw myself into the blinding headlights"; or they may be handled counterphobically and sadistically through arranging the death of others in reality or in fantasy, like the Marquis de Sade (Bach and Schwartz 1977). In any case, the passive longings for death usually contain a fantasy of reunion with the good mother.

At a more visible level, both the defensive omnipotence and the sadomasochistic enactments in which omnipotence is displayed are designed to ward off the horrible despair that recognition of the trauma would bring. While the treatment of sadomasochistic enactments is difficult enough, the exposure and reliving of this underlying despair make enormous demands on both patient and analyst, either or both of whom may prefer to abort the process. Let me give some examples to illustrate this.

A man who had been subjected to continual physical and emotional brutality throughout his childhood and adolescence had, by virtue of his courage and intelligence, managed to make a very happy and successful life for himself but never broke off relations with the parents who had abused and still continued to denigrate him. Behind this lay an omnipotent fantasy that somehow he would be able to change either himself or his mother so that, in the end, his mother would love him.

When at an advanced age an incident occurred that made the impossibility of this fantasy quite clear to him, he passed through a period in which he was highly suicidal and then for a long time he did nothing in his sessions but cry day after day.

This man once said to me: "When you're powerless as a child and you know there's nobody there to help you . . . the terror is if you can't do it . . . then you know you'll die cause everything depends on you. You're battling the death of yourself and the deep fear is that you won't come out of it and that you'll die in despair. . . . People need gurus, people who have been to places and come back alive with wisdom, because there's no other way you can know what things mean and you have to know what things mean. . . . "

This man was able to face the reality of his past history and overcome his despair, but it is not clear whether this ordeal can or should be traversed by everyone. Omnipotence is often a defense of desperation and deserves to be approached with a certain degree of prudence. In cases of omnipotence reactive to early childhood traumata, the first crack in the defensive wall may often be seen when the adult patient begins to develop psychosomatic symptoms and a sense that his body is fragile, vulnerable, or actually deteriorating. With certain more regressed patients, the psychosomatic symptoms may have always been present as a kind of endopsychic reminder that the denial of reality is only a plastered-over facade. With less regressed patients the psychosomatic symptoms may arrive as a frightening surprise when the patient finally regains touch with the earliest feelings of vulnerability that gave rise to his omnipotent defense.

Such patients may typically worry about cancer, their

organ systems, the aging process, their loss of sexual desire or sexual attractiveness, or they may simply have a foreboding sense of panic and doom. As this lost omnipotence slowly gets mourned and worked through, one sees a growing realization that time does not stand still but in fact passes, that people age and die, and along with this comes an increasing sensitivity to the hitherto unnoticed anniversaries, seasonal changes, and other traditions that mark our passage through life.

Let me give a final example from the supervision of a patient who was at the midpoint of this traversal, when he had recognized the loss of his omnipotence and the reality of death and had just reenacted his grief and despair about this in the transference. But he had not yet been able to connect this with the essential childhood trauma and to work through his despair. One day he remarked:

"Before I used to have fears that my body was ailing and I would run from one doctor to another because I wanted the doctor to say: *No! It's not there.* Now I feel that some part of my system is failing and I don't go to a doctor because I'm afraid that the doctor will say: *Yes! It is there.*"

T: [*"Before you wanted the doctor to say: 'No, death isn't there,' and now you're afraid that he'll say: 'Yes, death is there.'"*]

"You're right . . . I feel that the enemy has already gotten within the fort, like the Trojan horse . . . Before I used to feel so young, so strong, so powerful, and now I feel that no woman would ever look at me or find me attractive."

T: [*"Now you have death inside of you."*]

"Yes, I am damaged. Before I felt like some Apollo, eternally young, magical, androgynous, and now I feel tainted."

T: [*"The taint is that you're limited and mortal."*]

"But I used to worry so much about Death before, all the time, and now I hardly ever think of it."

T: [*"You used to feel like an immortal god but you worried about Death all the time; now you hardly think about Death, you just* feel *mortal."*]

"It used to feel so incredible that people grew up and became parents, I couldn't believe it. . . . Death is really the ultimate limitation. . . . In childhood I felt I could get away with anything, there were no limitations . . . I didn't have to do my schoolwork but I always got A's, I did the least work but got the most praise, I could have my pick of the girls . . . and now it's all crumbled. I don't feel I'm the greatest at anything, I'm just getting by . . . I used to be phenomenal, they always envied how lean and hard my body was, but now I think my flesh will deteriorate and I'll get fat and I'll die. . . . Before I would never even have thought of that because it never even occurred to me that anything like this would happen."

At this point the patient was still experiencing his loss of reactive omnipotence as a fall from a state of grace and perfection, a loss of androgyny, magic, and youth, and of the flawlessness of his body and mind. With time he would come to accept the indwelling of death, as we all must do.

But if we are to live without omnipotence and with death as a daily companion, what is there to save us from depression and despair? This touches on the difference between reactive omnipotence or manic defense and normal enthusiasm, passion, and creativity.

It is worth noting that whereas in omnipotence one believes oneself to have godlike powers or to be a God, in creativity or enthusiasm one is temporarily possessed by a God (en + theos), as the poets have so often expressed it. And perhaps this is merely another way of saying that whereas in omnipotence one is in a continuous state of subjective self-awareness, that is, unreflectively immersed in the experience of oneself, in enthusiastic or creative periods one may for a time be possessed by this state but ultimately must return to the more usual dialectical tension between subjective and objective self-awareness. This dialectic seems to imply not only an ongoing tension between our sense of aliveness and our reality testing, or between an overestimation of our powers and a tempering of that overestimation, but also a dialectical tension between life and death.

And it may well be our anxiety over this tension, one of the parameters of the human condition, that urges us on to seek some relief, some breakthrough, some transcendence of our human state, whether it be through ecstacy, through intoxications, through sadomasochistic perversions, or through some other transformations of the omnipotent pursuit of artificial paradises.

REFERENCES

Abelin, E. (1975). Some further observations and comments on the earliest role of the father. *International Journal of Psycho-Analysis* 56:293–302.

Akhtar, S., and Thomson, J. A. (1982). Overview: narcissistic personality disorder. *American Journal of Psychiatry* 139:12–20.

Amsterdam, B. K., and Levitt, M. (1980). Consciousness of self and painful self-consciousness. *Psychoanalytic Study of the Child* 35:67–83. New Haven, CT: Yale University Press.

Arlow, J. (1971). Character perversion. In *Currents in Psychoanalysis*, ed. I. Marcus, pp. 317–336. New York: International Universities Press.

Auerbach, J. S. (1990). Narcissism: reflections on others' images of an elusive concept (review essay). *Psychoanalytic Psychology* 7:545–564.

——— (1993). The origins of narcissism and narcissistic personality disorder: a theoretical and empirical reformulation. In *Empirical Studies of Psychoanalytic Theories: vol. 4. Psychoanalytic Perspectives on Psychopathology,* ed. J. M. Masling and R. F. Bornsteen, pp. 43–110. Washington, DC: American Psychological Association.

Bach, S. (1974). Notes on some imaginary companions. *Psychoanalytic Study of the Child* 26:159–171. New York: Quadrangle.

——— (1975). Narcissism, continuity and the uncanny. *International Journal of Psycho-Analysis* 56:77–86.

——— (1977). On the narcissistic state of consciousness. *International Journal of Psycho-Analysis* 58:209–233.

——— (1980). Self-love and object-love: some problems of self and object constancy, differentiation and integration. In *Rapprochement: The Critical Subphase of Separation-Individuation,* ed.

R. Lax, S. Bach, and J. A. Burland, pp. 171–197. New York: Jason Aronson.

———— (1985). *Narcissistic States and the Therapeutic Process.* New York: Jason Aronson.

Bach, S., and Schwartz, L. (1972). A dream of the Marquis de Sade. *Journal of the American Psychoanalytic Association* 20: 451–475.

Bak, R. C. (1968). The phallic woman: the ubiquitous fantasy in perversions. *Psychoanalytic Study of the Child* 23:15–36. New York: International Universities Press.

Balint, M. (1968). *The Basic Fault.* London: Tavistock.

Beckett, S. (1965). *Proust.* London: John Calder.

Beebe, B., and Lachmann, F. (1988). The contribution of mother-infant mutual influence to the origins of self and object representations. *Psychoanalytic Psychology* 5:305–337.

Beebe, B., and Stern, D. (1977). Engagement-disengagement and early object experiences. In *Communicative Structures and Psychic Structures,* ed. N. Freedman and S. Grand. New York: Plenum.

Bexton, W. H., Heron, W., and Scott, T. H. (1954). Effects of decreased variation in the sensory environment. *Canadian Journal of Psychology* 8:70–76.

Boesky, D. (1982). Acting out: a reconsideration of the concept. *International Journal of Psycho-Analysis* 63:39–55.

Bornstein, B. (1949). Analysis of a phobic child. *Psychoanalytic Study of the Child* 3/4:181–226. New York: International Universities Press.

Bower, G. (1981). Mood and memory. *American Psychologist* 36:129–148.

Brazelton, T. B., Koslowski, B., and Main, M. (1974). The origins of reciprocity. In *The Effect of the Infant on Its Caregiver,* ed. M. Lewis and L. Rosenblum. New York: Wiley–Interscience.

Breuer, J., and Freud, S. (1893–1895). Studies on hysteria. *Standard Edition* 3:1–306.

Broucek, F. (1991). *Shame and the Self.* New York: Guilford.

Bucci, W. (1985). Dual coding: a cognitive model for psychoanalytic research. *Journal of the American Psychoanalytic Association* 33:571–607.

———— (1989). A reconstruction of Freud's tally argument: a program for psychoanalytic research. *Psychoanalytic Inquiry* 9:249–281.

Chasseguet-Smirgel, J. (1983). Perversion and the universal law. *International Review of Psycho-Analysis* 10:293–301.

Chused, J. F. (1991). The evocative power of enactments. *Journal of the American Psychoanalytic Association* 39:615–639.

DeLoache, J. (1987). Rapid changes in the symbolic functioning of very young children. *Science* 238:1556–1557.

Dickes, R. (1965). The defensive function of an altered state of consciousness, a hypnoid state. *Journal of the American Psychoanalytic Association* 13:356–403.

Duval, S., and Wicklund, R. A. (1972). *A Theory of Objective Self-Awareness.* New York: Academic Press.

Eagle, M. N. (1984). *Recent Developments in Psychoanalysis: A Critical Evaluation.* New York: McGraw Hill.

Ellenberger, H. F. (1970). *The Discovery of the Unconscious: The History and Evolution of Dynamic Psychiatry.* New York: Basic Books.

Ellman, S. (1991). *Freud's Technique Papers: A Contemporary Perspective.* Northvale, NJ: Jason Aronson.

——— (1992). Psychoanalytic theory, dream formation, and REM sleep. In *Interface of Psychoanalysis and Psychology,* ed. J. Barron, M. Eagle, and D. Wolitzky. Washington, DC: American Psychological Association.

Emde, R. N. (1983). The prerepresentational self and its affective core. *Psychoanalytic Study of the Child* 38:165–192. New Haven, CT: Yale University Press.

——— (1988). Development terminable and interminable: I. Innate and motivational factors from infancy. *International Journal of Psycho-Analysis* 69:23–42.

Federn, E. (1953). *Ego Psychology and the Psychoses.* London: Imago.

Ferenczi, S. (1913). Stages in the development of the sense of reality. In *Sex in Psychoanalysis.* New York: Basic Books, 1950.

——— (1933). Confusion of tongues between adults and the child. In *Final Contributions to the Problems and Methods of Psychoanalysis,* pp. 156–167. London: Hogarth, 1955.

——— (1988). *The Clinical Diary of Sandor Ferenczi,* ed. J. Dupont. Cambridge, MA: Harvard University Press.

Fliess, R. (1953). The hypnotic evasion. *Psychoanalytic Quarterly* 22:497–511.

Freedman, N. (1994). More on transformation: enactments in psychoanalytic space. In *The Spectrum of Psychoanalysis: Essays in Honor of Martin Bergmann,* ed. A. Richards and A. Richards. New York: International Universities Press.

Freedman, N., and Berzofsky, M. (1994). Shape of the communicated transference in difficult and not-so-difficult patients: the symbolized and de-symbolized transference. *Psychoanalytic Psychology* (in press).

Freud, A. (1967 [1953]). About losing and being lost. In *The Writings of Anna Freud,* vol. 4, pp. 302–316. New York: International Universities Press.

Freud, S. (1900). The Interpretation of Dreams. *Standard Edition* 4–5:1–625.

_____ (1905). Three Essays on the Theory of Sexuality. *Standard Edition* 7:130–243.

_____ (1910). The antithetical meaning of primal words. *Standard Edition* 11:155–161.

_____ (1912). Recommendations to physicians practicing psychoanalysis. *Standard Edition* 12:111–120.

_____ (1914a). Remembering, repeating and working-through. *Standard Edition* 12:147–156.

_____ (1914b). On narcissism: an introduction. *Standard Edition* 14:73–102.

_____ (1915a). Observations on transference-love. *Standard Edition* 12:159–171.

_____ (1915b). The unconscious. *Standard Edition* 14:166–204.

_____ (1919). A child is being beaten: a contribution to the study of sexual perversions. *Standard Edition* 17:179–204.

_____ (1924). The loss of reality in neurosis and psychosis. *Standard Edition* 19:183–187.

_____ (1940 [1938]). Splitting of the ego in the process of defense. *Standard Edition* 23:275–278.

Gabbard, G. O. (1989). Two subtypes of narcissistic personality disorder. *Bulletin of the Menninger Clinic* 53:527–532.

Greenacre, P. (1968). Perversions: general considerations regarding their genetic and dynamic background. *Psychoanalytic Study of the Child* 23:47–62. New York: International Universities Press.

Grunes, M. (1984). The therapeutic object relationship. *Psychoanalytic Review* 71:123–143.

Hermann, I. (1976 [1936]). Clinging—going-in-search: a contrasting pair of instincts and their relation to sadism and masochism. *Psychoanalytic Quarterly* 45:1.

Isakower, O. (1963). Minutes of the faculty meeting. New York Psychoanalytic Institute, Oct. 14–Nov. 20. A. Z. Pfeffer, reporter.

Jacobs, T. (1986). On countertransference enactments. *Journal of the American Psychoanalytic Association* 34:289–307.

Jacobson, E. (1964). *The Self and the Object World.* New York: International Universities Press.

James, M. (1960). Premature ego development: some observations on disturbances in the first three months of life. *International Journal of Psycho-Analysis* 41:288–294.

James, W. (1896 [1984]). *William James on Exceptional Mental States,* ed. E. Taylor. Amherst, MA: Amherst University Press.

Kernberg, O. (1975). *Borderline Conditions and Pathological Narcissism.* New York: Jason Aronson.

Khan, M. M. (1979). *Alienation in Perversions.* New York: International Universities Press.

Kleeman, J. A. (1967). Peek-a-boo game: I: its origins, meanings, related phenomena. *Psychoanalytic Study of the Child* 22:239–373. New York: International Universities Press.

Klein, M. (1948). *Contributions to Psycho-Analysis 1921–1945.* London: Hogarth.

Kohut, H. (1971). *The Analysis of the Self.* New York: International Universities Press.

Lacan, J. (1949). The mirror stage as formative of the function of the I as revealed in psychoanalytic experience. In: *Ecrits: A Selection,* tr. A. Sheridan. New York: Norton.

Lachmann, F., and Beebe, B. (1992). Reformulations of early development and transference: implications for psychic structure formation. In *Interface of Psychoanalysis and Psychology,* ed. J. Barron, M. Eagle, and D. Wolitzky, pp. 133–153. Washington, DC: American Psychological Association.

Lakoff, G., and Johnson, M. (1980). *Metaphors We Live By.* Chicago: University of Chicago Press.

Lewin, B. (1948). The nature of reality, the meaning of nothing, with an addendum on concentration. *Psychoanalytic Quarterly* 17:524–526.

——— (1950). *The Psychoanalysis of Elation.* New York: Norton.

Lichtenberg, J. (1983). *Psychoanalysis and Infant Research.* Hillsdale, NJ: Analytic Press.

Lipton, S. D. (1977). The advantages of Freud's technique as shown in his analysis of the Rat Man. *International Journal of Psycho-Analysis* 58:225–274.

Loewald, H. W. (1960). On the therapeutic action of psychoanalysis. In *Papers on Psychoanalysis.* New Haven, CT: Yale University Press.

——— (1971). On motivation and instinct theory. In *Papers on Psychoanalysis.* New Haven, CT: Yale University Press.

——— (1978a). Primary process, secondary process, and language. In *Papers on Psychoanalysis.* New Haven, CT: Yale University Press.

——— (1978b). Instinct theory, object relations, and psychic-structure formation. In *Papers on Psychoanalysis.* New Haven, CT: Yale University Press.

——— (1980). *Papers on Psychoanalysis.* New Haven, CT: Yale University Press.

Mahler, M. S. (1972). Rapprochement subphase of the separation-individuation process. *Psychoanalytic Quarterly* 41:487–506.

Mahler, M. S., and McDevitt, J. B. (1982). Thoughts on the emergence of the sense of self, with particular emphasis on the body self. *Journal of the American Psychoanalytic Association* 30:827–848.

Mahler, M. S., Pine, F., and Bergman, A. (1975). *The Psychological Birth of the Human Infant.* New York: Basic Books.

McLaughlin, J. (1991). Clinical and theoretical aspects of enactment. *Journal of the American Psychoanalytic Association* 39:595–614.

Michotte, A. E. (1963). *The Perception of Causality.* New York: Basic Books.

Noll, R. (1992). *Vampires, Werewolves and Demons.* New York: Brunner/Mazel.

Novick, J., and Novick, K. K. (1991). Some comments on masochism and the delusion of omnipotence from a developmental perspective. *Journal of the American Psychoanalytic Association* 39:307–331.

Novick, K. K., and Novick, J. (1987). The essence of masochism. *Psychoanalytic Study of the Child* 42:353–384. New York: International Universities Press.

Opie, I., and Opie, P. (1969). *Children's Games in Street and Playground.* Oxford: Clarendon.

Peller, L. (1954). Libidinal phases, ego development and play. *Psychoanalytic Study of the Child* 9:178–199. New York: International Universities Press.

Piaget, J. (1945). *Play, Dreams, and Imitation in Childhood.* New York: Norton, 1951.

———— (1954). *The Construction of Reality in the Child.* New York: Basic Books.

Piaget, J., and Inhelder, B. (1956). *The Child's Conception of Space.* London: Routledge and Kegan Paul.

Pine, F. (1986). The "symbiotic phase" in the light of current infancy research. *Bulletin of the Menninger Clinic* 50:564–569.

Putnam, F. W. (1989). *Diagnosis and Treatment of Multiple Personality Disorder.* New York: Guilford.

———— (1992). Discussion: Are alter personalities fragments or figments? *Psychoanalytic Inquiry* 12(1):95–111.

Rapaport, D. (1951a). States of consciousness: a psychopathological and psychodynamic view. In *The Collected Papers of David Rapaport*, ed. M. Gill, pp. 385–404. New York: Basic Books.

———— (1951b). *Organization and Pathology of Thought.* New York: Columbia University Press.

Rilke, R. M. (1984). *The Selected Poetry of Rainer Maria Rilke* ed. and trans. by S. Mitchell. New York: Vintage.

Riva, M. (1993). *Marlene Dietrich by Her Daughter Maria Riva.* New York: Knopf.

Sade, D-A-F. (1986). *The Marquis de Sade: The 120 Days of Sodom and Other Writings,* comp. and trans. R. Seaver and A. Wainhouse. New York: Grove.

Sander, L. W. (1983). Polarity, paradox, and the organizing process in development. In *Frontiers of Infant Psychiatry,* ed. J. Call, E. Galenson, and R. Tyson, pp. 333–346. New York: Basic Books.

Sandler, J. (1960). The background of safety. *International Journal of Psycho-Analysis* 41(4):352–356.

Scholem, G. (1965). *On the Kabbalah and Its Symbolism,* trans. R. Manheim. New York: Schocken Books.

Schreier, H. (1992). The perversion of mothering: Munchausen syndrome by proxy. *Bulletin of the Menninger Clinic* 56:421–437.

Shelley, M. (1993 [1818]). *Frankenstein or the Modern Prometheus.* New York: Barnes & Noble.

Spitz, R. (1945). Hospitalism: an inquiry into the genesis of psychiatric conditions in early childhood. *Psychoanalytic Study of the Child* 1:53–74. New York: International Universities Press.

——— (1946). Hospitalism: a follow-up report. *Psychoanalytic Study of the Child* 2:113–117. New York: International Universities Press.

Stade, G. (1981). Introduction. In *Dracula,* by B. Stoker. New York: Bantam.

Stein, M. (1965). States of consciousness in the analytic situation. In *Drives, Affects, Behaviour,* vol. 2, ed. M. Schur. New York: International Universities Press.

Steingart, I. (1983). *Pathological Play in Borderline and Narcissistic Personalities.* New York: S. P. Scientific Books.

——— (in press). On language, action, love and the idea of reality.

Stern, D. (1983). The early development of schemas of self, other, and "self with other." In *Reflections on Self Psychology,* eds. J. Lichtenberg and S. Kaplan, pp. 449–484. Hillsdale, NJ: Lawrence Erlbaum Associates, Inc.

——— (1985). *The Interpersonal World of the Infant.* New York: Basic Books.

Stoker, B. (1981 [1897]). *Dracula.* New York: Bantam.

Stoller, R. (1988). Panel on sadomasochism in the perversions. American Psychological Association, December.

Suomi, S. J. (1991). Early stress and adult emotional reactivity in rhesus monkeys. In *Ciba Foundation Symposium 156: Childhood Environment and Adult Disease.* Chichester, England: John Wiley & Sons, Ltd.

Suskind, P. (1991). *Perfume: The Story of a Murderer*. New York: Knopf.

Tannen, D. (1990). *You Just Don't Understand: Women and Men in Conversation*. New York: Morrow.

Tomkins, S. S. (1963). *Affect, Imagery, Consciousness: vol. 2. The Negative Affects*. New York: Springer.

Waelder, R. (1930). The principle of multiple function: observations on overdetermination. In *Psychoanalysis: Observation, Theory, Application*, ed. S. Guttman. New York: International Universities Press.

Waldrop, M. (1992). *Complexity: The Emerging Science at the Edge of Order and Chaos*. New York: Simon & Schuster.

Walker, B. (1983). *The Women's Encyclopedia of Myths and Secrets*. San Francisco: Harper.

Weil, S. (1956 [1940]). *The Iliad, or The Poem of Force*, trans. M. McCarthy. Wallingford, PA: Pendle Hill.

Welldon, E. V. (1988). *Mother, Madonna, Whore: The Idealization and Denigration of Motherhood*. New York: Guilford.

Winnicott, D. W. (1962a). The theory of the parent–infant relationship: further remarks. *International Journal of Psycho-Analysis* 43:238–239.

_____ (1962b). Ego integration in child development. In *The Maturational Processes and the Facilitating Environment*. New York: International Universities Press.

_____ (1965). *The Maturational Processes and the Facilitating Environment*. New York: International Universities Press.

_____ (1966). Comment on obsessional neurosis and "Frankie." *International Journal of Psycho-Analysis* 47:143–144.

_____ (1971). *Playing and Reality*. New York: Basic Books.

_____ (1984). *Deprivation and Delinquency,* eds. C. Winnicott, R. Shepard, and M. Davis. London: Tavistock.

Wolff, P. H. (1987). *The Development of Behavioral States and the Expression of Emotion in Early Infancy*. Chicago: University of Chicago Press.

INDEX

About the Author

Sheldon Bach received his Ph.D. in Clinical Psychology from New York University, where he was a National Institute of Mental Health Research Fellow. He interned at Jacobi Hospital and was on the staff and visiting staff of Jacobi and Montefiore Hospitals and a member of the faculty of the Albert Einstein College of Medicine for twenty years. He is currently Clinical Professor of Psychology at the New York University Postdoctoral Program in Psychoanalysis, a training and supervising analyst at the New York Freudian Society, a Fellow of the Institute for Psychoanalytic Training and Research, and a member of the International Psychoanalytical Association. Dr. Bach is in full-time private practice in New York City.

27740874R00121

Made in the USA
Lexington, KY
21 November 2013